Direct Investment
and European Integration

CHATHAM HOUSE PAPERS

A International Economics Programme Publication
Programme Director: J. M. C. Rollo

The Royal Institute of International Affairs, at Chatham House in London, has provided an impartial forum for discussion and debate on current international issues for some 70 years. Its resident research fellows, specialized information resources, and range of publications, conferences, and meetings span the fields of international politics, economics, and security. The Institute is independent of government.

Chatham House Papers are short monographs on current policy problems which have been commissioned by the RIIA. In preparing the papers, authors are advised by a study group of experts convened by the RIIA, and publication of a paper indicates that the Institute regards it as an authoritative contribution to the public debate. The Institute does not, however, hold opinions of its own; the views expressed in this publication are the responsibility of the authors.

CHATHAM HOUSE PAPERS

Direct Investment and European Integration
Competition among Firms and Governments

**Stephen Thomsen and
Stephen Woolcock**

The Royal Institute of International Affairs

Pinter Publishers
London

Pinter Publishers Limited
25 Floral Street, Covent Garden, London WC2E 9DS, United Kingdom

First published in 1993

© Royal Institute of International Affairs, 1993

British Library Cataloguing in Publication Data
A CIP catalogue record for this book is available from the British Library

ISBN 1-85567-118-2 (Paperback)
    1-85567-117-4 (Hardback)

Typeset by Koinonia Limited
Printed and bound in Great Britain by
Biddles Limited, Guildford and King's Lynn

To Sandy and Margaret
and
Edie and Archie

CONTENTS

Contents

TABLES AND FIGURES

Tables and figures

Boxes

PREFACE

The International Economics Programme of the Royal Institute of International Affairs has followed closely the explosion of foreign direct investment that has occurred since the early 1980s. At the same time, the European Programme has taken a keen interest in the process of European integration, particularly the Single European Market. This study, funded by the Ford Foundation, was an attempt to bring together these two strands of research in the context of direct investment and European integration. Not only is the role that direct investment plays in European integration often largely ignored, but discussion of the increasing foreign investments of European firms within their own market has often been limited to mergers and acquisitions activities, with scant regard for the valuable information provided in the statistics on direct investment. In this book, we look at how European firms have responded to greater integration, where obstacles remain to further integration through FDI, and what effect these investments will have on the future shape of the European economy.

We have benefited greatly from a series of study groups that were held at Chatham House throughout 1992. Their constructive and detailed review of our research has significantly improved both the content and the presentation. Also thanks to those in Brussels and Paris and at the Danish Summer Research Institute who took the time to discuss the draft text. Jim Rollo, as Head of the International Economics Programme at the RIIA, was responsible for the overall management of the project. His encouragement and efforts to keep the project on schedule are gratefully acknowledged, as is the advice of Pauline Wickham, and work by Margaret May and Simona Lyons in preparing the manuscript. The views expressed in this book are those of the authors and should be attributed neither to the RIIA nor to the Ford Foundation.

S.T.
January 1993   S.W.

1

INTRODUCTION

Direct investment among the richest countries has been one of the salient features of the world economy since the mid-1980s.[1] Within this broad trend, Europe featured prominently as both a home and host to multi-national enterprises (MNEs). Not only did many Japanese and American firms invest massively, but even the most somnolent European firms appeared to awake to the need to look beyond their own national borders. Figure 1.1 shows just how dramatic this growth in foreign direct invest-ment (FDI) has been for Europe. In spite of the attention that Japanese investment has received in both Europe and North America, it pales in significance compared with the activities of European MNEs both at home and in the United States.

For almost all European countries for which data exist, both inflows and outflows of FDI played a greater role in their economies in the second half of the 1980s than at any time since the formation of the original Common Market. In the first phase of this internationalization, European firms invested heavily in the United States, which was growing more quickly and offered a large and lucrative market. In the past few years, their attention has turned towards the European market. The 1980s thus represented a strong break with the past in terms of European integration. The growing intra-EC trade and American FDI in Europe which had characterized the first three postwar decades suddenly gave way to new and more varied patterns of both trade and investment. The greatest change occurred in the flourishing overseas investment activity of Euro-pean MNEs.

Previous studies by the Royal Institute of International Affairs, such as Julius and Thomsen (1988), have found that FDI is highly cyclical and no

1

Figure 1.1 European outward investment, 1971–91

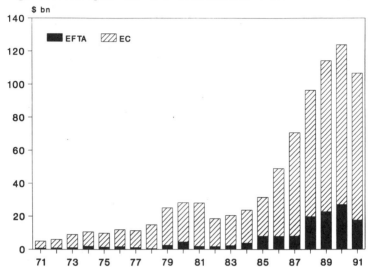

doubt the business cycle contributed to the rapid growth and subsequent contraction observed in Figure 1.1. But behind this cycle a number of structural changes influenced firms' behaviour, particularly the rapid pace of technological change and increasing competition from Japan and the newly-industrializing countries (NICs). European firms also faced deregulation, privatization and liberalization of their domestic economies as well as greater global integration through negotiations on trade and investment in GATT and the OECD. Within the European Community, the Single Market initiative vigorously attacked the competitive status quo. The effect of these changes was universal, encompassing virtually all countries and industries within Europe.

In narrow terms, FDI is simply all capital transferred between a firm and its new or established foreign affiliates. In its broadest sense, FDI represents competition: among workers, governments, firms, markets and even economic systems. European integration will intensify all forms of competition, and direct investment patterns provide a foretaste of potential outcomes. Foreign direct investment is not something that lends itself to easy generalizations. Strong statements must always be qualified by saying that some industries are exceptions to the rule or that a particular outcome is by no means guaranteed. In this book, we focus on the role that FDI can play in enhancing competition within the European market. We recognize, however, that cross-border acquisitions may sometimes represent an oligopoly in search of a monopoly, and our policy conclusions will incorporate this possibility. But rather than reciting this liturgical caveat each time pro-competitive effects are suggested, we defer this discussion to the end and focus instead on those aspects of FDI that are less well appreciated.

We also make no recourse to case-studies, though we recognize their usefulness in providing insights about firms' behaviour. Readers interested in case-studies of European industries should consult Mayes (1991). Where differences across sectors affect our conclusions, we will discuss them, but in general we will resist any temptation to present individual industries or firms. Our motives are not just epistemological; evidence from studies of direct investment as well as some of our own research presented here suggests that differences across industries in terms of where and why they invest are not as great as is commonly assumed. Rather than describing individual industries, we discuss the various parameters such as economies of scale or product differentiation that make firms behave differently.

Chapter 2 begins with a description of general European trends in terms of direct investment, along with some discussion of the variation that one observes across Europe in levels of both outflows and inflows. Chapter 3 looks at three possible motives for this increase in MNE activity in Europe. The first examines FDI from the perspective of mergers and acquisitions, using the analysis typically applied in a domestic context. The other two motives relate to the question of why a firm would want to locate some production or other activities in another European country. One reason relates to the benefits of lower wages (adjusted for productivity) or more favourable government policies. This strategy is behind the assumption that direct investment patterns in Europe represent a relocation of economic activities within the Single Market. The second reason for wanting to produce abroad stems from the advantage that it provides in terms of market proximity, suggesting that FDI has more to do with competition than it does with actual resource transfers.

Chapter 4 examines the patterns of investment in Europe in the light of these three possible motives. It is, of course, difficult to ascribe exact motives to investors simply on the basis of where they choose to invest, but the evidence is consistent enough to allow us to make some quite firm generalizations. When investing abroad, firms look for large or neighbouring markets. The importance of market size suggests that market proximity plays a part in firms' strategies, regardless of whether the affiliate is meant to serve only the local market or the whole European market. The tendency to invest in neighbouring countries, on the other hand, suggests that the prospects for a genuine regional division of labour encompassing the whole European market may be limited. European firms appear to invest either next door or way beyond their own continent in the largest markets or where the most productive and cheapest workforces can be found. They are, in turn, most likely to receive investment from these same countries, the net result being a good deal of cross-hauling of investment, often within the same industry.

Chapter 5 asks what role government policies play in influencing the location of economic activity within the European Community. The evidence suggests not only that incentives have a limited effect on firms' decisions but also that regulatory arbitrage through FDI is not likely to bring sufficient pressure to bear on countries to lead to a harmonization of policies, except in a few cases. Chapter 5 also addresses the question of structural barriers to investment and whether they will remain even within the Single Market. These structural barriers, such as public procurement practices which favour domestically owned firms, often impede both trade and investment. Others relate specifically to FDI, such as the difficulty in making a hostile bid in much of continental Europe – a difficulty that will persist even after implementation of the Single Market. Policy recommendations are presented in the concluding chapter.

Two themes appear again and again throughout the book. The first is the notion that much of the direct investment within Europe represents an increase in competition among firms as they venture beyond their own sheltered markets. The second is the way in which governments must compete more and more through their policies to attract footloose firms. While targeted policies designed to entice investors may fall short of expectations, it is clear that in the long run the macroeconomic and microeconomic policies that a country adopts will have a crucial impact on its attractiveness as a location for firms.

Competition among firms

In our discussion of the effects of FDI, we suggest that such investment supplements and often exceeds exporting as a way of increasing market share abroad. This process began with American MNEs in the 1960s and 1970s and has now been taken up by Japanese and European firms. The ubiquitous presence of US MNEs in Europe in the 1960s prompted fears

Figure 1.2 US exports and direct investment to Europe

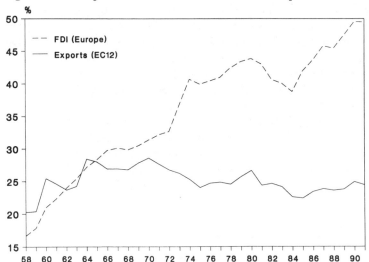

of economic hegemony which reached their peak in *The American Challenge* by J.-J. Servan-Schreiber (1967). Figure 1.2 looks at the share of total US exports and FDI going to Europe since 1958. The export share grew rapidly in the early 1960s as economic growth in Europe partly offset any diversionary effect from the common external tariff, but it has fallen slightly since then. In contrast, the share of US FDI going to Europe has grown every year, except for a brief relapse in the early 1980s. As a result of this growing divergence between exports and local production as a way of serving the European market, US-owned firms in Europe now sell almost five times as much locally as America exports to Europe. Perhaps not surprisingly, the greatest source of transatlantic trade tension is in those sectors in which there has been very little FDI, such as agriculture, aircraft or steel. American goods sold in Europe are most likely to be produced there.

Within Europe it is more difficult to assess the extent to which firms sell in one another's markets through local production rather than exports. There is no reliable source of information on intra-EC direct investment that would allow us to make the comparison between trade and local sales. While intra-EC trade grew no more quickly than world trade, direct investment by European firms flourished in the 1980s. Thus it seems likely that exports as a percentage of total foreign sales have fallen for European firms as well.

5

The threat of competition, together with the growing sophistication of products and consumers, means that firms must place a greater emphasis on market proximity. Increasingly in many industries, exporting has become a second-best option. Market share rivalry requires a local presence achieved through direct investment in the local market. Hence, competition among firms through direct investment is becoming more and more crucial in ensuring that the gains from the Single Market are achieved.

This aspect of international competition is not adequately reflected in the 1992 programme. While cross-border mergers and acquisitions are expected to facilitate European industrial restructuring, the competitive impetus for this change is expected to come from greater intra-EC trade. Virtually no mention is made of direct investment, whether from within or outside the EC. One of the aims of this study is to place the rapid growth of direct investment in Europe during the 1980s in the context of European integration and to define more clearly those barriers to intra-European direct investment which still impede European integration. Many of these barriers are buried deep within the structure of each national economy.

As commerce has evolved, so too has commercial policy – both globally and within the EC. Initiatives within the EC often mirror and sometimes precede GATT negotiations. Overall, there does appear to be a progression through various fora towards a more catholic view of market access. As tariffs have been reduced in successive GATT rounds, awareness has grown of the importance of non-tariff barriers (NTBs). During the Tokyo round of GATT, for example, efforts were made to limit the distorting effects of national domestic policies, i.e. those NTBs with a fairly direct impact on trade, such as the promotion of national industries through subsidies, preferential purchasing or technical standards.

The assessment of such non-tariff barriers is still relatively straightforward in that they are more or less directly related to trade, but increasingly it has become apparent that domestic regulatory policies may also hinder imports. Unlike most NTBs, these seldom have trade restriction as their objective, but the differences between national regulatory regimes mean that companies wishing to gain effective access to a market have to invest within that market. This was particularly the case in the field of services, resulting in their inclusion in the Uruguay round of GATT and a redoubling of efforts to establish effective codes for capital movement and national treatment within the OECD. The desire to establish multilateral disciplines on investment policies also found expression in the inclusion of a specific negotiating group on trade-related investment measures (TRIMs) in the Uruguay round.

Before policy-makers could devise a multilateral agreement covering certain aspects of regulatory barriers to trade, another impediment was pushed onto the policy agenda, i.e. structural factors, most clearly exemplified by the US–Japanese Structural Impediments Initiative (SII). What is at issue is not the discriminatory action – whether knowingly, as in the case of tariffs, voluntary restraint agreements (VRAs) or subsidies, or less obviously with regulatory barriers to trade – but the absence of action by national authorities. Possibly the best example is the lack of intervention by national competition authorities to break down restrictive market structures in order to create a more competitive and transparent market. Hence the discussion of the need for some multilateralization of competition policies.

Thus as investment has increasingly become the medium for international exchange, the range of barriers which might figure in commercial policy has increased. The GATT has tried to enlarge its ambit through its work on TRIMs, but the share of global investments directly affecting exports of the host country is quite small. The important barriers to investment are not performance requirements but rather structural impediments within the host country. Similarly, the inclusion of investment issues relating to services overlooks the extent to which manufacturers engage in overseas production as a means of expanding market share, irrespective of the barriers to exports.

Competition among governments

If investment barriers are the counterpart of barriers to imports, then policies which seek to induce inward investment are comparable to subsidies which foster domestic production at the expense of foreign locations. Each policy seeks to distort competition to the advantage of one country. In Chapter 5, we identify the range of government policies which affect the attractiveness of individual countries within Europe. Competition among governments must also be considered in a broader context than simply competitive subsidization. Government policies and economic systems have always competed, whether through armed struggle or by means of trade. Successful policies of one government are imitated elsewhere, just as privatization has become *de rigueur* in countless developed and developing countries. Anglo-Saxon and Continental forms of capitalism are continually reassessing their efficiency in the light of each other's experience.

Direct investment has made this competition more immediate. A country which does not enact business-friendly policies risks losing its firms to locations elsewhere through an exodus of direct investment. Similarly, countries that do not compete actively to attract investment may deprive themselves of vital technologies as well as management and marketing skills. Because firms can respond quickly to changing policies through direct investment, these flows may provide a foretaste of the future location of various economic activities throughout Europe.

Firms may well respond to these incentives or to differences in regulations across Europe, but at the same time it must be recognized that direct investment need not involve any actual transfer of resources from one country to another apart from financial capital. If an investor buys a local firm, the immediate effect is nothing more than a change of ownership. Furthermore, direct investment among industrialized countries is usually a two-way flow, often within the same industry. As such it is competition among firms, not governments. It is vital for our purposes to distinguish between net flows and cross-hauling of investment between countries.

Too often, inflows or outflows are interpreted in too narrow a context without any appreciation for the underlying factors behind FDI flows. Michael Heseltine, president of the Board of Trade, warned recently that 'Britain could lose its position as a favourite location for inward investors into the EC unless it appeared to be an enthusiastic supporter of the Community'.[2] At the same time, adoption of the Social Chapter would allegedly diminish this role. While the British government attributes its success in attracting inward investment to policy initiatives, other countries emphasize their low labour costs. Germany worries that it will lose factories to lower-wage locations such as Spain, while Spain and Portugal fret about the appeal of Eastern Europe to north European firms in search of export platforms. This debate rages not only at a regional level but also at a global one. Some American academics such as Reich (1991) have claimed that EC policies are designed to attract investment away from the US towards Europe. Government policies clearly have an effect on investment flows and hence on the location of economic activity in Europe, but in many cases this role is grossly exaggerated. One aim of this study is to examine the exact role of different national and EC policies in shaping the pattern of investment as well as to discuss the extent to which low labour costs and other sources of comparative advantage appeal to investors.

Conclusion

Intra-Community direct investment does not occur in a vacuum; it must be seen against the backdrop of an ever-increasing internationalization of business which affects virtually all countries and industries. We hesitate to refer to such a trend as globalization, since the term conjures up images of firms released from the bonds of geography and hence is at odds with the more prosaic reality of FDI. Although our focus is on direct investment in Europe, principally by its own firms, we must always remember that the growth of direct investment is not confined to Europe. The European market nevertheless provides an interesting microcosm of changes under way at a global level. The fact that Europe has relatively few barriers to trade should allow us to isolate more carefully the range of non-trade policies which affect investment. Europe also incorporates a range of different national economic and policy environments: from the high-cost locations of Germany and the Netherlands to low-cost Spain and Portugal; from the liberal policy environment of northern Europe to the more restrictive France and Italy; from the active competition policies of Britain and Germany to the absence of any effective competition policy in Italy or Greece; finally from the Anglo-Saxon approach to capital markets in Britain to the less liberal markets elsewhere on the continent.

2

TRENDS IN DIRECT INVESTMENT IN EUROPE

The European Community is the world's largest direct investor, representing roughly one-half of OECD outflows since 1980. If EFTA countries are included, then European outflows accounted for almost two-thirds of OECD flows in 1991. As a location for investment, however, Europe's historical role as host to American firms was usurped by record levels of inward investment in the United States from both Europe and Japan. Only since 1988 has Europe managed to regain its status as the world's foremost recipient of direct investment. The significance of Europe in global direct investment is often overlooked amidst all the excitement generated by Japanese and American MNEs.

European Community direct investment has two dimensions: intra- and extra-EC flows. It is difficult in practice to distinguish between the two. Some extra-EC FDI may actually be destined for another EC country or for the home country, as is the case with some Italian investment in Switzerland or Dutch flows to the Netherlands Antilles, both of which represent significant outflows. Nevertheless, Eurostat figures for the period 1984–9 do permit some qualified conclusions. Even if we exclude intra-EC flows, the Community was the world's largest direct investor until 1989, when Japan edged ahead. Flows into the Community, however, were barely one-fourth of those going to the United States over that period. As a result, the Community as a whole was a substantial net overseas investor until 1989, when both intra-EC investment and non-EC inflows caught up with extra-EC outflows (see Figure 2.1). In other words, in 1989 roughly one-half of total EC direct investment remained within the Community. Net outflows from the EC have been very much a

Figure 2.1 EC direct investment

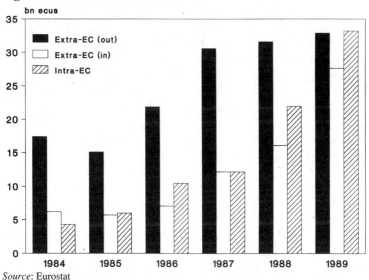

Source: Eurostat

function of Community investment in the US, accounting for almost three-quarters of extra-EC investment, only slightly offset by net inflows from EFTA countries and Japan. In spite of all the attention that Japanese investment in Europe has received, it has been greatly exceeded by direct investment by firms from EFTA. The surplus with the US represented a historic reversal that would have been considered inconceivable 25 years ago when Servan-Schreiber warned in *The American Challenge* of the economic colonization of Europe by American MNEs.

The fact that Europe invested four times as much in America as it received in the second half of the 1980s is partly a reflection of the maturity of the US presence in Europe. By and large, American MNEs did not retreat from Europe. Rather, many US firms have already achieved such a substantial presence in the regional market that they are content to grow through the retained earnings of existing affiliates. If one considers only the actual capital sent by the parent firm, then EC flows to the US have been 11.5 times higher than US flows to the EC since 1987. Because many European MNEs came of age in the 1980s, much of their investment in the US was new investment paid for by the parent firm. Indeed, for the past three years, retained earnings of European-owned firms in the US have been a negative $20 billion as a result of losses on their US operations stemming in part from the recession. Recent figures

11

reveal a dramatic decline in European investment in the US, down from $43 billion in 1989 to only $8 billion in 1991. This suggests that some sort of equilibrium stock of FDI in America may have been reached, although the recession in both America and parts of Europe no doubt contributed greatly to this fall. The divergence in the age of American and European investments may help to explain the strong surplus in favour of Europe, but it cannot account for the fact that the initial impact of the drive towards the Single Market was to push EC firms into the American market. Whether this move had anything to do with the process of European integration cannot be understood until we have discussed motives for FDI in the next chapter.

In 1989, for the first time, intra-Community flows exceeded those with non-EC countries. As we can see from Figure 2.1, the most dramatic increases in direct investment in the late 1980s were in intra-Community flows and in investment into the Community. This growth and its implications for Europe will be an important focus of the rest of the book. Given the wide margin of error at such an aggregate level, we should be cautious in our comparisons. With the decline in outward flows by Britain in 1991, the link with the outside may have been reduced substantially and it seems likely that we will see an even more impressive increase in the intra-Community share when the most recent figures become available.

Discussing the EC member states together as a group is useful because it allows us to distinguish between external and internal flows. But the total EC figure is an aggregated figure which hides important variations within the Community. These variations in regional versus external flows for major European countries can be seen in Table 2.1. The outlier in terms of both inflows and outflows is clearly Britain; to a lesser extent, Ireland is too, for much the same reason. While between one-half and two-thirds of most European countries' investment remains in Europe, the European share of British FDI is only 28 per cent. The same is true for inflows: investment in Britain comes equally from the US and the rest of Europe, while for other European countries (excluding Ireland) investment comes predominantly from Europe.

Table 2.1 also provides some idea of the relative stocks of inward and outward investment for these countries. The exact levels must be taken with a pinch of salt as no two countries record investment in exactly the same way and the time periods involved also differ. Nevertheless, the orders of magnitude are such that we can state with some certainty that Britain dominates both inward and outward investment in Europe. When

Table 2.1 Global patterns of European investment (percentage of stock in or from each region)

Inflows	From: US	Japan	Europe	Total stock* (bn ecus)
To:				
Belg.–Lux.	14	6	71	28.0
France	12	6	75	48.4
Germany	30	7	56	68.0
Ireland	50	3	41	na
Italy	14	2	80	44.8
Netherlands	27	4	66	53.0
Portugal	8	2	80	6.3
Spain	8	3	81	67.8
Sweden	10	na	87	8.9
UK	41	5	39	153.3
Europe	27	5	60	478.4
Outflows	To: US	Japan	Europe	Total stock* (bn ecus)
From:				
Denmark	14	1	72	7.8
France	25	0	62	63.0
Germany	23	2	55	112.9
Italy	9	1	68	47.1
Netherlands	31	1	66	78.7
Sweden	14	na	74	3.3
Switzerland	23	na	53	47.7
UK	39	1	28	163.0
Europe	27	1	53	549.7

*Some countries do not record stock figures. In these cases, cumulative flows were used.

we consider also that much of this British investment involves the US rather than Europe, it becomes clear that the extra-EC flows described earlier are in large part a British phenomenon, with the Netherlands playing a strong supporting role.[1] Other European countries are naturally also eager to invest in the US, but almost always less than in the rest of Europe. The UK represents 41 per cent of European investment in the US and 17 per cent in Japan. In many Commonwealth countries the British share is probably even higher.

Britain is not only the Community's largest outward investor, it also

Trends in direct investment in Europe

Table 2.2 Outflows as a percentage of GDP

%	1960–69	1970–79	1980–89	1990–91
4.51–5.0				Sweden
4.01–4.5				Netherlands
3.51–4.0				Belg.–Lux (90)
3.01–3.5			UK	
2.51–3.0				Switzerland (90)
2.01–2.5			Netherlands Sweden Switzerland	Finland
1.51–2.0	Switzerland	UK		France Norway UK
1.01–1.5	Netherlands	Netherlands Switzerland	Belg.–Lux. Finland Norway	Austria Denmark Germany
0.51–1.0	UK	Germany Sweden	Denmark France Germany	Austria Spain
0.0–0.5	Austria Belg.–Lux. Denmark Finland France Germany Italy Norway Sweden	Austria Belg.–Lux. Denmark Finland France Italy Spain	Austria Italy Spain	Italy

takes in the lion's share of external investment into the EC. Unlike other Community members, the UK receives more investment from outside the EC than it does from within. Britain is rarely the first location for investors within the Community, but it clearly is for Japanese, American and Swedish firms, as well as for investors from Commonwealth countries such as Canada. Britain's overriding importance in total EC inflows is therefore a function of its long-established role as a gateway to the rest of Europe for firms investing from outside the Community. If Britain is indeed a 'Trojan horse' by allowing non-EC firms to gain access to the EC through its market, then it has been so for a very long time. Furthermore, there is no evidence yet of any dwindling fondness for Britain as a host country on the part of non-European firms. American manufacturing

14

Table 2.3 Inflows as a percentage of GDP

%	1960–69	1970–79	1980–84	1985–89	1990–91
4.01–4.5					Belg.–Lux. (90) Portugal (90)
3.51–4.0					
3.01–3.5					
2.51–3.0					UK
2.01–2.5				Belg.–Lux.	Netherlands Spain
1.51–1.5				Portugal Spain UK	Greece (90) Sweden Switzerland (90)
1.01–1.5	Belg.–Lux. Netherlands	Belg.–Lux. Ireland Netherlands Norway UK	Belg.–Lux. Greece Ireland UK	Greece Netherlands	Denmark
0.51–1.0	Denmark Germany Italy Norway Switzerland UK	Greece Portugal Spain Switzerland	Netherlands Spain Switzerland Portugal	France Norway Sweden Switzerland	Finland France
0.0–0.5	Austria Finland France Spain Sweden	Austria Denmark Finland France Germany Italy Sweden	Austria Denmark Finland France Germany Italy Norway Sweden	Austria Denmark Finland Germany Ireland Italy	Austria Germany Ireland (90) Italy Norway

investment in Germany may be catching up with that in Britain, but in service sectors the UK still takes in almost one-half of American direct investment in the Community. Japanese firms continue to pour into Britain in spite of the oft-professed need to spread their activities throughout the EC, if only for political reasons.[2]

Because of the difficulties in distinguishing between intra- and extra-Community flows, we will focus in what follows on total outflows and inflows from individual European countries as a way of determining some of the broad characteristics of active home and host countries. In spite of the universal nature of direct investment, there are nevertheless important differences across countries and industries which may help us to understand some of the underlying causes, both general and specific, of the increase in FDI.

Tables 2.2 and 2.3 show outflows and inflows from individual countries as a percentage of GDP, providing a rough measure of the relative importance of FDI to each country by removing the effects of both inflation and overall economic growth. For almost all European countries, both inflows and outflows represented a higher percentage of GDP in the late 1980s that at any time in the past three decades. The slowing down of economic growth in Europe beginning in 1990 has managed only partially to reverse this trend. Such uniformity in investment behaviour is astonishing given the diversity in market size and structure and in regulatory regimes across Europe.

Outflows by country

Table 2.2 reveals that although all countries appear to have become greater outward investors, there are nevertheless important differences across Europe in terms of the propensity to invest abroad. What might account for this variation? At first glance, there is little to distinguish active home or host countries from marginal ones. Some small countries such as Sweden, the Netherlands and Switzerland figure prominently as outward investors, while others including Denmark, Austria, Greece, Portugal and Ireland do not. One reason for this variation among small countries is simply their undiversified industrial base. Given the size of their markets, smaller countries usually concentrate on only a few sectors, and because the propensity of firms to become MNEs differs greatly across sectors, the industrial composition of these countries will influence their potential to serve as a home to MNEs. A handful of firms can generate enormous amounts of outward direct investment, and it should not come as any surprise that Sweden, the Netherlands and Switzerland all possess such firms. Electrolux, Unilever and Nestlé are only a few examples.[3] Denmark or Ireland, with their strengths in food production, are less likely to become major outward investors.

To explain this variation in outward FDI among small countries would require an understanding of why countries have developed certain industries instead of others, a question which is no doubt partly explained by the historical and actual comparative advantage of each country. What about the larger countries? Presumably they are not constrained by an undiversified industrial base, so why are some large countries insignifi-

Table 2.4 Market capitalization and FDI outflows (per cent)

Country	I	II
UK	43.2	32.9
Germany	13.8	15.0
France	12.4	13.1
Switzerland	6.6	7.2
Netherlands	4.9	8.9
Spain	4.6	1.3
Italy	4.4	4.5
Sweden	4.3	8.6
Belgium–Luxembourg	2.5	3.3
Denmark	1.3	1.0
Norway	0.7	1.6
Austria	0.4	0.3
Ireland	0.3	0.0
Finland	0.3	2.3
Portugal	0.1	0.1
Europe, total	100	100

I Share of each country in total market capitalization of the 500 largest firms in Europe (based on market capitalization) as recorded by *The Financial Times*. In those cases where the company has two distinct national identities, the capital is divided evenly between the countries.
II Share of each country in total European FDI outflows from 1970 to 1990.

cant as outward investors? Outflows from the UK were twice as high as from Germany or France in the late 1980s and five times as high as from Italy, although levels have appeared to converge in 1990–91. Part of the reason for the variation is simply that Britain has two of the world's largest oil companies and the petroleum sector has traditionally been an active overseas investor. Here, once again, historical developments influence present outflows. But even if we exclude the oil sector, Britain is still by far the largest outward European investor.

One reason may relate to industrial structure. Italy and Germany, for example, have many small and competitive firms producing and exporting differentiated products of high quality in low volumes, such as textiles and machine tools. Many of these firms are family-owned. State ownership has also acted as a restraint on outward investment although the French public sector has become active in foreign acquisitions, partly owing to encouragement from the French government. The role of market structure is suggested in Table 2.4, which compares total outflows from 1970 to 1990 for each European country with that country's share in

17

the total market capitalization of the 500 largest European firms (FT 500). The smaller countries which are active overseas investors also contribute far more to the total market capitalization than those countries which do not figure prominently in outward investment. The FT 500 list includes state-owned companies in which private investors hold at least 25 per cent of the stock, as well as subsidiaries of larger groups as long as outside investors hold 25 per cent. The direction of causality between market capitalization and FDI outflows is difficult to assess: market capitalization may result from MNE activity and not the other way round. Nevertheless, the correlation between the two is clear and should serve as a reminder in later chapters that although thriving capital markets make it easier for hostile takeovers from abroad, they also provide a ready source of funds for outward investment.

In spite of traditional divergences in the level of outflows from individual European countries, levels do appear to be converging somewhat, although it is dangerous to look for trends at a time of such volatility in flows. Not only has the leading role of the United Kingdom been usurped by Germany and France, but Italy has also witnessed growing levels of overseas activity by its own firms. Such events will depend critically on the ways in which governments' policies to liberalize, deregulate and privatize their economies interact with corporate strategies to diversify or to expand abroad.

Inflows by country

Inflows are a different story altogether. The issue of why firms choose to invest in some countries more than others and the ability of governments to influence those decisions has strong economic and political implications. It will be one of the main focuses of future chapters. For the moment, we merely wish to describe some of the differences among host countries in terms of their ability to attract investors, and to discuss changes over time.

Table 2.3 on inflows shows some similarities with Table 2.2 on outflows, particularly the spectacular growth registered in inflows for many European host countries. Nevertheless, there are important discrepancies in the role played by foreign firms in individual countries. The UK ranks far above other large European countries, and the Netherlands, Switzerland and Sweden also figure prominently. As we might expect, some of the same characteristics of countries that encourage outflows (e.g. capital markets and industrial structure) also draw in investment from abroad. But the inflows side is also a good deal more complex. If we look instead at absolute levels of inward investment in the Community, the dominant role of Britain is readily apparent: it represents 40 per cent of all inflows in the 1980s, which is more than Germany, France, Italy and Spain combined. Once again, the oil sector is important, particularly the Anglo-Dutch company Royal Dutch/Shell, but Britain is equally important in manufacturing.

In contrast to the flourishing foreign business community in the UK, Germany appears as a bulwark against incursions by foreign firms. For the largest economy in Europe to receive only six per cent of EC inflows in the 1980s is astonishing and has sparked fears of an industrial exodus from Germany in the face of rising labour costs, a strong currency and stringent environmental regulations. Without discussing firms' motives for investment we cannot assess this claim, but there is reason to doubt it even on empirical grounds. While the Bundesbank reports that American MNEs have actually withdrawn $1.2 billion since 1986, the US Commerce Department records continuing investments worth $9.4 billion by US firms in Germany during that period.[4] This discrepancy should serve as a warning against using unreliable FDI statistics as a basis for policy without a thorough understanding of what they mean and how they might be inaccurate. Nevertheless, an earlier study by the RIIA (Julius and Thomsen, 1988) found that foreign involvement in Germany is less than in either Britain or France by various indicators.

Net flows

One of the questions that we wish to address in this study is the extent to which direct investment within Europe represents a relocation of economic activities in the wake of increased integration. Net flows for individual countries should provide a rough idea of whether this is occurring. As one might expect, capital-rich countries that are home to MNEs, such as Sweden, Britain, the Netherlands and Germany, have traditionally been strong outward investors on a net basis. Relatively labour-abundant countries such as Spain, Portugal, Ireland, Greece and even Belgium–Luxembourg are all traditional net recipients of investment. Other countries either have no pattern or have seen a reversal in trends over time. France shifted from a net recipient in the 1970s to a major outward investor in the 1980s. Italy saw both record net inflows in 1987 and record net outflows in 1991.

Table 2.5 shows the net position for each European country in terms of

Table 2.5 Net flows of European direct investment, 1987–91

Country	Net flow (m ecus)	Country	Net flow (m ecus)
Germany	52,976	Italy	1,435
Sweden	38,793	Ireland	-402
France	37,802	Greece	-3,707
Switzerland	21,687	Belg.–Lux.	-4,856
UK	20,454	Portugal	-5,281
Netherlands	17,631	Spain	-36,282
Finland	12,199		
Norway	4,630	EC12	82,277
Denmark	2,507	EFTA	79,756
Austria	2,446	Europe	162,033

cumulative flows since 1986. Germany stands out as the country with the greatest net outflows, followed by Sweden and France. The fact that so many European countries have more outward than inward investment relates partly to net investment of 50 billion ecus in the United States during that period, though that still leaves a substantial net outflow unaccounted for. Some of this obviously went to developing countries, but since the late 1980s witnessed a dramatic decline in such flows it is an insufficient explanation. The International Monetary Fund (1992) records substantially higher outward than inward investment at a global level, which suggests that the creditor status of Europe may be partly a statistical discrepancy. We have already seen a $10.6 billion discrepancy between German and US sources for American investment in Germany over that period.

Net flows can also be highly volatile. Britain, for example, sent abroad record net outflows of 16 billion ecus in 1988. This represented the culmination of a decade of uninterrupted net outflows, exceeding those even of Germany. By 1990, the balance had shifted to net inflows of 14 billion ecus. Are we to interpret this as a dramatic shift in the attractiveness of the UK as a location for investment? Clearly not. Similarly, for Sweden, continually climbing net outflows throughout the 1980s reached a peak of 16 billion ecus in 1990 but then fell to only 1 billion ecus the following year. These examples demonstrate that from one year to the next, the level of net inflows or outflows can reverse itself, even if the country has a long history of outward investment. To design policies based on the present balance is a risky enterprise.

Figure 2.2 EC mergers, manufacturing

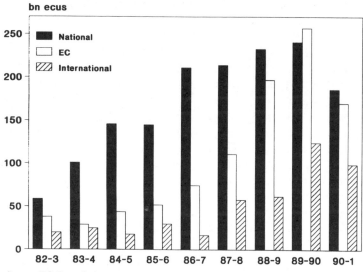

Source: EC Commission.

Figure 2.3 EC mergers, services

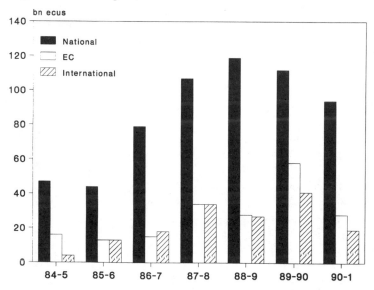

Source: EC Commission.

Mergers and acquisitions

A large share of direct investment in Europe occurs through mergers and acquisitions (M&As). Japanese firms tend to prefer greenfield sites and many peripheral countries attract new factories, but these appear to be the exceptions. Evidence from the United States shows that acquisitions have represented 85 per cent of the total value of foreign investment in the US over the past five years, with the rest going to new establishments. If, as we argue in later chapters, direct investment in Europe is principally for the purposes of market access, then it is equally likely that acquisitions dominate the European figures as well, since market access is often best achieved by acquiring a local firm with knowledge of that market.

Most of the statistics on mergers and acquisitions come from information provided in financial newspapers. Figures 2.2 and 2.3 depict M&A activity involving the 1,000 largest EC firms in manufacturing and services. The mergers are divided among those involving two firms from the same country (national), those among firms from two different member states (EC), and those in which a Community firm is acquired by a firm from outside the EC (international). All three types of mergers reached a peak at the end of the 1980s and then fell off in the early 1990s, but the growth of national mergers occurred in the early part of the decade, while cross-border mergers grew more quickly in the latter part of the 1980s. In 1989–90, for the first time, the largest EC manufacturing firms were more acquisitive abroad than at home. Figure 2.3 suggests that a slight lag between national and foreign mergers also existed in the service sector, though national mergers still exceed foreign ones.

The geographical pattern of mergers and acquisitions closely follows that of FDI, as one would expect if M&As are the main medium through which FDI occurs. Thus in recent years France has been the most aggressive acquirer of companies in other countries, with an annual average of $12 billion in acquisitions in other member states in 1989–91, followed by Britain ($5.5 billion average) and Germany ($5 billion average). At the same time, British firms have been the most popular targets, with an average of $19 billion in foreign acquisitions in the UK, followed by France ($6 billion average) and Germany ($5 billion average). The M&A figures support the view that French companies are rapidly internationalizing in order to catch up after a period in which French industry was excessively nationally focused.

The low level of acquisitions of German firms and the popularity of UK firms appears to support the view that the openness of the domestic capital market determines the prevalence of mergers, but we must be

Table 2.6 Intra-Community cross-border M&As by sector, 1984–91

	84–5	85–6	86–7	87–8	88–9	89–90	90–1	Total
Chemicals	23	28	27	38	56	75	53	300
Food	1	7	11	18	27	44	26	134
Paper	5	4	7	6	26	30	11	89
Construction	1	2	3	12	19	17	27	81
Metals	3	1	4	9	13	28	16	74
Electronics	5	0	6	4	18	15	14	62
Machinery	4	3	8	5	17	13	2	52
Transportation	2	0	6	9	6	13	9	45
Extractive	0	3	1	2	5	8	5	24
Textiles	0	1	2	2	7	8	3	23
Computers	0	0	0	1	0	1	0	2
Other mfg.	0	3	0	5	3	4	4	19
Banking	6	4	3	12	16	23	13	77
Insurance	7	3	7	14	8	18	7	64
Distribution	3	6	5	8	4	17	8	51

Source: Annual Report on Competition Policy, EC Commission, Brussels.

cautious in drawing this conclusion. While an active and open capital market makes acquisitions easier, it also imparts a bias to cross-country comparisons. The values mentioned above are based only on mergers for which a value was reported. Because acquisitions in Britain are often of companies quoted on the stock exchange while those in other countries sometimes involve private companies, the value of acquisitions of UK firms is more likely to be public knowledge than when a private continental company is acquired. If we eliminate this bias by looking at the total number of acquisitions instead of the reported values, the British share of total acquisitions between 1988 and the first half of 1992 falls from one-half in value terms to one-quarter in terms of the number of acquisitions.

Data on mergers also allow us to look more closely at the industrial composition of recent investment activity. Table 2.6 looks only at foreign mergers involving two EC firms and shows that in almost all sectors intra-EC mergers were far greater at the end of the decade than five years earlier. The chemical industry alone represented over 25 per cent of the total, followed far behind by food products with 12 per cent. These two sectors accounted for almost one-half of all manufacturing mergers. Nevertheless, virtually all sectors witnessed a rapid increase in mergers over the decade. Only in the computer industry, which is characterized by large national champions, were EC mergers negligible.

Conclusion

In this chapter, we have merely presented the 'facts', though we hesitate to describe FDI statistics in that way. Given the political importance attached to inward investment, the inadequacy of the figures provided by national governments should be an acute embarrassment. The European Commission is moving at an evolutionary pace towards more common methodologies but convergence is no quicker than in other spheres. Nevertheless, there are some general points that we can extract from the available sources. The first is the dominant role of the UK in total flows both from and to the Community. In contrast, France is currently most active within the EC while Germany is a major investor yet appears to receive little inward investment. In spite of these variations, there does appear to be some convergence. The British stranglehold on external flows has weakened in the past two years as the UK flows have fallen and other countries have recently become major investors.

We have not tried to explain why the UK is the first choice of outside investors nor why Germany appears as a reluctant host country except to suggest the obvious correlation with the domestic capital market. We have also not tried to distinguish among the various possible influences of integration on investment in new member states. All the issues are best understood once we have analysed motives for direct investment. Only then can we make sense of both the changing pattern of investment in Europe and its implications for national economies and for Europe as a whole.

3
MOTIVES FOR DIRECT INVESTMENT IN EUROPE

Foreign direct investment is driven by a multitude of causes, which in turn affect the European economy in manifold ways. In some cases it is a result of increased integration, in others a reaction to the lack of integration. Direct investment sometimes involves a transfer of production to a foreign location, but at other times it has no effect on resource allocation between the two countries. For these reasons, we eschew any attempt to fit recent trends into simple generalizations, focusing instead on three distinct motives for FDI which we believe are prevalent in Europe. All three motives focus on the efficiency gains from FDI. We will leave for Chapter 6 the important question of possible anti-competitive strategies involving FDI, as well as any discussion of the interaction between these firm-level strategies and European integration.

Greater integration, such as through the removal of non-tariff barriers as part of the 1992 programme, is supposed to lead to a Single Market in which firms sell in a non-discriminatory manner throughout the Community. The analogy is often made with the United States. In such a market, where differences in factor costs, government regulations, etc. still exist, firms have an incentive to seek out the lowest-cost location in which to produce. After all, they can, in principle, serve the whole market from anywhere within the Community. At the same time, the integrated market offers greater scope for economies of scale for individual firms. Rather than trying to expand output by wresting sales away from rivals in other markets, firms may opt for the quicker route of merging with former rivals in order to reap the benefits of greater output in the shortest possible time. These mergers show up potentially as FDI.

In both of these cases, integration allows firms within the market to lower their production costs and hence to become more competitive at home and abroad. In neither case is FDI essential, but given the range of entry and exit barriers that hamper such restructuring, both are likely to be orchestrated partly within or by MNEs.

The third broad motive for FDI has little to do with restructuring but rather represents a market-oriented growth strategy in which direct investment is preferred over exporting as a means of selling goods and services in other member states. The growth in such market-based FDI can be explained by the firm's need to expand beyond its own national market both to grow and to defend against incursions into its own market.

In what follows, we describe in more detail the motives behind these three strategies, leaving to the next chapter any assessment of their relative importance in explaining direct investment in Europe. Admittedly, the distinction among the three is somewhat contrived. A firm may acquire a foreign rival in order to gain economies of scale, lower costs of production and access to that market. It is likely that the acquisition by Volkswagen of SEAT of Spain fulfils all three criteria. What matters is the weight attached to each motive. The reason for making this distinction among investment strategies is simply that each implies a different configuration of European industry in the future. We will begin with FDI as a form of industrial restructuring through cross-border M&As.

FDI as a form of industrial restructuring
Industries are in constant flux. Not only does demand expand and contract both cyclically and secularly, but new technologies can rapidly transform the nature of the industry itself. Governments also play a role, for instance by removing regulations which artificially separate two different industries or firms in different regions or by controlling monopolistic tendencies of firms. In some industries the government has also been the chief customer, so policy changes can significantly alter demand. When demand contracts, firms are no longer able to rely on overall market growth and must compete more vigorously to fill excess capacity. New technologies favour first movers and upset the status quo in industries. The elimination of government-imposed entry barriers and NTBs allows for more competition both from other countries and from firms in other industries. This competition forces firms to adapt to the new environment.

Irrespective of the exact origin, industrial restructuring did occur in Europe in the 1980s, much of it through mergers among firms within the same national market. For reasons that are poorly understood, these mergers often tend to occur in waves, and the M&A activity that took place in Europe in the late 1980s was the fourth such wave this century. It was also the first time that mergers spilled over borders to any great degree, with the largest EC manufacturing firms making more acquisitions abroad than at home in 1990. When these acquisitions are financed from the home country, they are recorded as FDI. Geroski and Vlassopoulos (1990, p. 44) argue that 'increases in cross-border merger activity occur when increases in total merger activity deplete the stock of attractive domestic partners enough to make it worthwhile for merger active firms to begin to seek out partners abroad.'

European Commission studies have suggested that this industrial restructuring through cross-border mergers is the main reason why direct investment has increased within the Community and is directly attributable to the advent of the Single Market. As Hager and Wolf (1988, p. 27) explain:

> transborder business activity is a pre-condition for the functioning of
> a modern exchange economy. Its relationship to the overall 1992
> project is therefore one of an accelerator or inhibitor of the positive
> effects, both static and dynamic, expected from trade and services
> liberalisation in general. As such it is a parameter to be put before
> the entire welfare function established for the 1992 project.

The Commission expects that one-third of the gains from the Single Market, or roughly 60 billion ecus, will come through economies of scale (80 per cent of which will be achieved through restructuring and only 20 per cent through increases in output). These gains will vary widely across industries, but in some cases may be significant. The authors of the Cecchini Report (1988) claim that a doubling of output in refining and car production would reduce unit costs for supplementary production by 10 per cent. In aircraft manufacture the reduction would be closer to 20 per cent.

In spite of these rather straightforward calculations, the possibility of unexploited scale economies is by no means widely acknowledged. Geroski (1991, p. 20) cites the Commission's own figures to suggest that 'most of the industries surveyed (89 per cent of them) exhibited levels of minimum efficient scale less than 10 per cent of the Community market, and three quarters were less than 5 per cent.' These levels, he argues, hardly provide the basis for claiming that EC firms are too small. 'Furthermore, the penalty to sub-optimum efficient scale production was found to be fairly modest in most sectors, leading one to suspect that most markets could sustain at least twenty efficient producers, and often considerably more.' Estimates of potential scale economies usually measure what is technically feasible and ignore any kind of managerial limitations. Geroski and Jacquemin (1985, p. 302) observe that large firms are often more strike-prone and tend to be less innovative. They suggest that productivity differences are explained much less by differences in the size of establishments than by differences in labour relations, training, and the availability of skilled workers. European firms are already often of equal size to American firms, and both tend to be significantly larger than Japanese firms.

There are clearly certain sectors which stand to gain from scale economies in Europe even if the majority may not. Are these sectors the ones which have witnessed the most cross-border activity in recent years? Here, once again, there is reason to doubt the importance of restructuring as a motive. As Geroski and Vlassopoulos (1990, p. 29) argue, 'In as far as European industry ought to be restructured to reduce excess capacity and exploit scale economies, the sectoral patterns of mergers that we observe seem to be somewhat out of line with independent assessments of where rationalization ought to occur.'

The chemicals and food sectors together account for 40 per cent of all mergers involving EC firms and almost one-half of cross-border mergers, as we saw in Table 2.6. A recent study by de Ghellinck (1991, p. 369) of the chemicals sector found that 'since the late 1970s, there has been an unending cycle of mergers, takeovers, R&D and marketing cooperation agreements, and exchanges of shares, divisions and equipment, but it is difficult to see which of these activities have taken place in response to setting up of the Single Market in 1992.' To the extent that there is restructuring under way in the chemical industry, it is global, not regional. European chemical firms are already the largest and most competitive in the world. The same is true in the food sector, where three European firms are among the four largest worldwide. Many of the acquisitions have been of small firms supplying local brands in each market as a way of filling up costly distribution and manufacturing capacity by adding new products. Unilever made 100 acquisitions for $2.5 billion in the 1980s.[1]

Another way to gain insights into the difficulties involved in restructuring and how these are affected by the Single Market is to look at the experience of individual firms that are already pan-European in terms of their operations. How integrated are their various national subsidiaries and what determines the degree of integration? The tension that managers of individual firms face between flexibility at a national level and efficiency at a European one is the firm-level equivalent of the barriers to European restructuring at the industry level. In what follows, we present evidence of a few pan-European firms. We do not pretend that they are necessarily representative of European industry as a whole; selective case-studies can be used to support any hypothesis. Rather, we merely wish to suggest that the potential for Europe-wide rationalization is sometimes unaffected by the level of non-tariff barriers in Europe.

Firm-level rationalization
The propensity of firms to rationalize their operations across countries depends very much on what they produce, and to whom they sell. Government policies clearly play a role in this regard. Public procurement practices which favour locally-based firms encourage MNEs to keep subsidiaries in more countries than can be justified on efficiency grounds alone. Cantwell (1992a, p. 222) notes that very little rationalization, whether intra- or inter-industry, has occurred in the defence procurement sector for example. Differing standards within the Community in terms of labelling, packaging, etc. also make it more difficult for firms to adopt regional product-based strategies. The Cecchini Report (1988, p. 62) argues that these barriers to both inter- and intra-company rationalization are significant and that 'so-called "inherent" divergences in customer requirements may be largely a case of national tastes determined by national regulations'. *Ipso facto*, by removing national regulations that restrict trade and hence hinder rationalization, the Single Market will encourage industrial restructuring in Europe partly through FDI. The mergers that have occurred in Europe in the past five years are seen as a vindication of this approach.

Although trade barriers no doubt discourage rationalization, two examples of individual firms illustrate why too much focus should not be placed on the role of such obstacles. Ford, the American automobile manufacturer that first invested in the UK before the First World War, began to rationalize its operations in Europe as early as 1967. Dicken (1992, p. 300) illustrates how production of the Ford Fiesta in the late 1970s was divided among at least 15 countries, not only in the EC and EFTA but also Japan, Canada and the United States. The transportation sector is one in which economies of scale can be enormous, so Ford's strategy is not surprising. What is surprising is that it began to rationalize as early as

1967, given the state of European integration 25 years ago. Barriers to trade may prove to be an obstacle, but in some industries at least they are not an insurmountable one. Indeed, it has been a source of frustration for some Europeans since Servan-Schreiber in *The American Challenge* that US firms have managed to take more advantage of the opportunities of the integrated European market than their local competitors.[2]

The second example comes from the food sector, which has been the second most active after chemicals in terms of mergers and acquisitions. A Commission study in *European Economy* (1990, p. 5) cites the example of Unilever, which between 1973 and 1989 rationalized its production of detergents from nine plants to only four. For such a firm in an industry where consumers are highly brand-conscious and where brands differ across countries, tension between flexibility and efficiency is particularly acute. Rationalization of operations is constrained not by governments but by consumers. As Cantwell (1992a, p. 220) explains, 'national differentiation prevails in sauces and biscuits, in which integration is liable to fail, while differentiated customer sets or products types running across EC countries can be identified in the markets for coffee and cereals, in which integrated EC strategies are feasible'. Even with coffee, however, national tastes can differ slightly. Nestlé, for example, provides 52 different varieties of its brand Nescafé.[3]

The influence of trade barriers depends very much not only on the industry but on the particular good in question. In some cases, rationalization has not been hindered as much by governments as by managerial inertia, and here the Single Market may exert a strong effect in forcing firms to rethink their existing structure. In other cases, rationalization could not occur even within a perfectly integrated market simply because differences in national tastes are too great. At the expense of greater production efficiency, European firms learn to adapt their products to differing national tastes. To imply in this case that market fragmentation places European firms at a disadvantage in global markets is surely misplaced. The flexibility that European firms have learned at home may well be one of the reasons why they are among the largest in the world food industry.

We have presented circumstantial evidence to suggest that looking at cross-border M&As solely as a form of restructuring leaves many questions unanswered. In some industries the removal of trade barriers is neither a necessary nor a sufficient cause for restructuring. If industrial restructuring is seen as necessary, then the Commission might want to attack more directly the various entry and exit barriers that thwart mobility and change. Removing trade barriers merely creates more opportunities for restructuring; it does not by itself bring about that restructuring. Even within national markets, where trade barriers do not pose a threat, exit barriers may exist. In the German steel industry, for example, exit barriers have hampered much-needed rationalization among the four large producers.

Industrial restructuring of the kind described above often involves mergers or acquisitions. When these are financed in the home country of the acquiring firm, they are recorded as FDI. Not all M&As are financed in this way, of course, but the mere fact that both cross-border M&As and direct investment registered unprecedented increases in the late 1980s suggests a fair amount of overlap. Because until recently such mergers occurred primarily in a domestic context, the analysis of merger motives has not incorporated much of a foreign component. Consequently, most studies of intra-European mergers have looked to industrial causes stemming from the Single Market. A study by the London Business School (1990) is one noteworthy exception. The rest of our book will focus on FDI rather than on cross-border mergers because we believe that foreign investment activity within Europe is part of a *location* strategy of firms. In contrast to the economic literature on mergers, much of the work on FDI arose out of the need to explain why a firm would choose to produce abroad rather than simply exporting. FDI theory is therefore more appropriate when discussing the location strategies of firms in Europe and how this may change as the economies become more integrated. We turn now to these location strategies.

A regional division of labour within Europe?

A regional division of labour requires labour costs adjusted for productivity to differ within Europe. To what extent is this the case? The internal market and in particular the elimination of capital controls (with temporary exemptions for certain poorer members) has meant that the EC is fairly close to full free movement of capital, while labour remains largely immobile across borders within the Community. Language, culture and practical issues, such as education and pension rights (where compatible systems do not yet exist) all contribute to this lack of mobility. Partly as a result, labour costs differ widely within the Community, though they are converging slowly over time for many countries.

Labour costs are comprised of three components: wages, non-wage costs such as social security contributions by employers and other social

Motives for direct investment in Europe

Figure 3.1 Comparison of hourly wage levels and labour costs in Europe, 1990

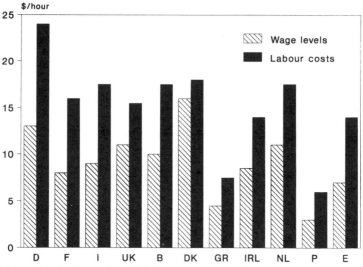

Source: London Economics/LE/MES.

provisions, and productivity. Figure 3.1 compares wage rates across the EC, converted into dollars at the current market exchange rate, and shows German wages to be four times higher than those in Portugal. In general terms the EC member states fall into three groups: a high-wage group consisting of Denmark, western Germany, Belgium and the Netherlands, where wage rates are between 110 per cent and 190 per cent of the EC average; a middle group consisting of Britain, France and Ireland, where the average national wage rates range from 70 per cent to 120 per cent of the EC average; and the low-wage group including Italy, Spain, Greece and Portugal, with between 35 per cent and 80 per cent of EC wage rates. In spite of these differences, there has been significant convergence over the past 20 years. The exceptions to this trend have been Greece, which after some convergence has fallen away again during the 1980s, and Portugal, which has yet to begin significant convergence. Spain has converged considerably over two decades, EC membership appearing to contribute to this towards the end of the 1980s.

Labour costs are dependent not only on wage rates negotiated, whether through binding tariff agreements as in Germany or free collective bargaining as in most other countries, but also on non-wage labour costs. These vary between 100 per cent of wage costs in Italy, owing to

32

Table 3.1 The structure of labour costs in manufacturing (%)

	D	F	I	NL	B	L	UK	IRL	DK	GR	E	P
Total labour costs	100	100	100	100	100	100	100	100	100	100	100	100
Direct wages	56	52	53	56	54	69	71	70	83	62	—	59
Non-wage costs	44	48	47	44	46	31	29	30	17	38	—	41
of which:												
Social security	21	28	33	24	24	15	14	15	6	18	—	18
Paid holiday	11	9	11	10	9	11	10	12	8	7	—	5
Other non-wage	12	11	3	10	13	6	5	3	3	13	—	18
Non-wage as % of wage	77	90	87	78	82	45	40	43	20	63	—	70

Source: Eurostat, 'Labour Costs'.

generous pension and social security provisions, and 20 per cent of wage rates in Denmark, where social security expenditure is paid for through taxation rather than separate contributions. There is no correlation between high wages and high non-wage labour costs. Denmark has high wages but very low non-wage costs, Italy falls into the lower group on wages and Britain and Ireland, which are around the middle of the EC wage spectrum, are towards the bottom of the non-wage labour cost spectrum. Figure 3.1 shows that when one considers hourly labour costs the range is less broad. Germany is still the highest-cost location ($24/hour) but Italy, Belgium, the Netherlands and Denmark are close behind (at around $19/hour). Britain, France, Spain and Ireland follow ($14-16), with Portugal and Greece trailing. In view of the efforts to harmonize certain social provisions in the EC it is important to be aware of how the non-wage labour costs are comprised. The most important factor, as seen from Table 3.1, is statutory social security payments (32 per cent of total labour costs in Italy compared with 5 per cent in Denmark or 7 per cent in Britain) and paid holiday (about 10 per cent across the EC).

The final element of the labour cost calculation is productivity. Countries with higher wages such as Germany are able to offset some or all of this difference through higher levels of productivity. When productivity rates are combined with labour costs to give unit labour costs, or the costs of producing a unit of output, one finds that the divergences among locations are virtually eliminated, at least among the central member states. Nevertheless, an investor can sometimes achieve productivity levels in the host country that far exceed those of the average firm. A detailed survey of the world motor industry (Womack et al. 1990, p. 87) found that Ford's plant at Hermosillo, Mexico had the best assembly-plant quality of all plants that the authors inspected, including Japanese-owned plants in Japan and North America. To the extent that this is true for other industries as well, then the relevant variable is labour costs and not unit labour costs. There will, of course, always be a need for at least a minimum of infrastructure and workers' skills, but clearly the periphery of Europe fulfils these requirements in large measure.

Given that wage differentials provide scope for a regional division of labour in Europe, to what extent is it likely? Evidence from investment in the periphery of Europe will be provided in the next chapter. While the Commission has high hopes for cross-border mergers, it does not expect much of a shift in the location of value-added activities within the Community. The authors of a Commission study on social Europe in *European Economy* (1990, p. 4) predict that 'The completion of the single market should ... neither upset the mix of sectoral specialisations across member states nor lead to massive transfers of economic activities between geographic zones.' Not only are lower wages often offset by lower levels of productivity, but the Commission also provides evidence that EC countries are already specialized in their intra-EC trade on the basis of comparative advantage. It is commonly assumed that intra-industry specialization poses fewer adjustment costs than the inter-industry variety, so it is perhaps not surprising that the Commission plays down the potential for greater inter-industry specialization. Greenaway and Hine (1991) offer an opposing view. They find that while production patterns became more similar in the 1970s, implying that the Community was moving away from inter-industry specialization, the trend was reversed between 1980 and 1985.

As trade barriers come down within Europe as part of the 1992 programme and with the admission of new members, there will be greater scope for specialization. In addition to this static reallocation of resources within the EC, there are dynamic changes within countries and industries which ensure that the best place to produce a particular good may change over time. Technological leaders in one decade may be followers in the next. Industries that were once well-suited to the comparative advantage of a country might become more labour- or capital-intensive over time. As industries and countries evolve, disfavoured industries migrate to more favourable climes not only within Europe but worldwide.

The traditional way to see whether integration has led to increased specialization within Europe has been to look at inter-industry trade flows. Of necessity this can only be seen after the event. A quicker alternative is to observe the location decisions of firms in Europe. There is no reason to believe that MNE strategies within Europe will yield any different outcome from what would have occurred had no FDI taken place. If Portugal is the best place to produce shoes within the Community, then it will attract other European shoe producers as well as stimulating its own domestic shoe industry. In both cases, exports of shoes from Portugal increase. Nevertheless, it is possible that shifts in production occur more quickly when orchestrated within the MNE than they would otherwise, especially if there are entry barriers or market imperfections to trade which make it hard for domestic firms to take advantage of the new opportunities offered by integration. Foreign direct investment will therefore foreshadow the regional reallocation of resources within Europe to reflect the greater degree of economic integration among national economies.

Chapter 4 will provide evidence of whether firms are promoting greater inter-industry specialization among the member states. Unfortunately, it is difficult to know what this regional division of labour should look like and, more importantly, whether FDI statistics capture this trend. The peripheral countries offer unskilled labour, while Germany is rich in human capital. Some investors will choose one type of location and some the other, depending on their products and the techniques they favour. To see whether the pattern of FDI is consistent with comparative advantage, we would have to look at individual industries, but most national governments provide only a rough industrial disaggregation of the data. Nevertheless, we can make broad distinctions between services and manufacturing, as well as drawing on survey research of MNE motives and market orientation in various countries. Before that, we must be clear about why firms would invest abroad if the comparative advantage of the host country were not the main motivation.

Motives for market-based FDI

Dunning (1977) has clearly identified three conditions for direct investment to take place. First, a firm must have some firm-specific or intangible asset such as proprietary technology or managerial or marketing expertise that allows it to compete with local firms in each market; second, the firm must have a reason for wanting to use this asset abroad rather than at home; and third, it must also decide that control over production is better than simply licensing the technology or intangible asset. These three conditions are known respectively as ownership, location and internalization. Our interest is in the location advantages of producing in the local market, though it must be kept in mind that they do not by themselves guarantee that a firm will invest abroad unless the other two conditions have already been fulfilled.

Why might a firm prefer to produce locally in a market instead of exporting from another location? Exporting is difficult in some industries because of high transportation costs or because of the perishability of the good. Roughly 80 per cent of EC food is still processed in the country in which it is consumed. In many service industries, exporting is simply not an option as the buyer and seller must be in the same place at the same time. Although there are obvious cases such as tourism where the buyer goes to the seller's market, it is more often the case that the service firm invests in the local market, particularly in accounting, advertising, consulting services and distribution. Table 3.2 compares direct exports and

Table 3.2 Foreign revenues of US service firms ($bn)

	Direct exports	Affiliate sales	Total
Accounting	0.2–0.5	3.7–4.0	3.9–4.5
Advertising	0.1–0.5	1.7	1.8–2.2
Data processing	0.1–1.2	2.5–3.7	2.6–4.9
Engineering	1.1–1.6	4.0	5.1–5.6
Insurance	2.7–3.6	10.1–12.1	12.8–15.7
Retailing	0.0	25.4	25.4
Telecommunications	1.3	1.3	2.6
Transportation	17.1	10.9	28.0
Travel	14.1	0.0	14.1

Source: McCulloch (1988), extracted in Sapir (1991).

local sales of US service companies. In many cases, the ratio of local affiliate sales to US exports is higher than in manufacturing, and in some sectors there are no exports. The growth of the service sector in national economies and the increasing international competition in services may explain why the share of services in total FDI is growing over time, as remarked by Julius (1990, p. 32). Services are also often heavily regulated, so even when a local presence is not essential on commercial grounds, the firm may be induced to invest in order to comply with local regulations. Furthermore, ownership advantages may resemble public goods in that, once developed, they do not need to be re-established in every market in which they sell, especially when the buyers are clients from the investing country who have also expanded abroad.

The case for market-based FDI in manufacturing is more nuanced, but the same principles apply. Not only are many goods differentiated across countries and thus close contact with the consumer is advisable, but the manufacture and sale of these goods also involves a considerable number of service transactions. Product differentiation is often put forward as the primary cause of the rapid expansion of intra-industry trade within Europe following (though not necessarily caused by) European integration in the late 1950s. Just as product differentiation leads to intra-industry trade, it may also lead to FDI. Caves (1971) and others have suggested that FDI is most likely to occur in differentiated product industries because local goods are not perfect substitutes for those of the investing firm and thus the investor is sheltered from local competition. Furthermore, differentiated products require greater flexibility, an increased awareness of how local tastes differ in each market, and in general a greater effort at marketing, distribution and after-sales service – all characteristics that are required when selling products abroad which are not completely accepted or understood by local consumers. Indeed, the greatest push towards differentiation in manufacturing may be through related services rather than through the goods themselves. Not only do individual consumers require more attention to marketing and greater assurances of reliability and quality, but industrial customers demand speed of delivery such as in just-in-time systems, greater innovation upstream and a closer relationship between supplier and industrial user.

For many firms wishing to sell in developed markets abroad, exporting may increasingly become a second-best option. Not all firms are large enough to engage in FDI, while others are restricted by plant-level economies of scale, but as product and service differentiation continue and as the service sector expands, the tendency for firms to invest directly for market access will grow. Direct investment will not supplant trade, which has been growing steadily over the past five years along with FDI. Rather, local production will exceed exports because it allows firms to expand market share beyond what could be achieved through exports alone. Costs of production do not need to be lower in the host country if total revenue is also higher. The exact conditions under which profitability will be higher with local production depend on the cost differential, which is a function of relative factor costs and economies of scale in each market, and on what happens to prices when firms compete more directly. It is certainly possible to envisage a situation in which local production expands revenue more than costs, thus increasing the profits of the investor. As research by Haigh et al. (1989, p. 7) on location decisions within the United States has shown, 'a firm interested in maximising its profits would search not just for a site with the lowest costs, but for a location that would maximise the difference between revenues and costs.'

Another reason why static cost comparisons may not be decisive arises when there are potential first mover advantages. In such circumstances, foreign takeovers will be preferred over both exports and greenfield investments abroad. The firm which acquires another firm more quickly than its rivals makes market access more difficult for them in turn. By making a quick acquisition rather than, for example, investing in a distribution network in order to increase exports, the investor is able to expand its market share in the host country overnight. The French chemical company Rhône–Poulenc was able to reduce its dependence on the French market for health product sales from 75 per cent to 33 per cent in one year through acquisitions abroad.[4]

The role of trade policy
In spite of these compelling commercial reasons for a local presence, direct investment is typically seen as a reaction to trade policy. American firms in the 1960s and Japanese companies in the 1980s supposedly invested in Europe to counter the uncertainty over EC trade policy. The correspondence in time between shifts in EC policies and inward investment into the EC has lent support to this hypothesis. At the same time, the removal of internal barriers as part of the Single Market initiative is widely regarded as the driving force behind cross-border M&As in Europe in the late 1980s, as firms restructured to take advantage of greater cost savings through economies of scale. The failure to restructure earlier is attributed to the lack of a credible commitment to the Single Market.

While trade policies no doubt played a role in all of these cases, they fail to explain a number of issues. Why, for example, did US FDI into EFTA countries (excluding the UK) grow faster than into the EC following the Treaty of Rome in 1957? Why is Japanese FDI into the EC still so much smaller than into the US in spite of the fact that the EC may be the more protectionist of the two? Similarly, if trade barriers had previously prevented the restructuring of European industry, then why are many American firms already pan-European? Why did national and international mergers grow along with European ones in the 1980s? Why, if European restructuring was at the heart of these mergers, did so much European investment flow to the United States following the White Paper on the Single Market in 1985? These questions all point to the need to look beyond shifts in EC trade policy as the driving force behind direct investment in Europe.

A synthesis
Production can be rationalized on a Europe-wide basis, either by consolidating in a particular location or by distributing the various activities according to factor cost and regulatory differences across Europe. A third possible strategy is to relocate closer to consumers, whether in individual markets or within the Single Market itself. These three strategies were discussed separately in this chapter though clearly they are all interrelated. We now wish to bring the strands of our analysis back into a common framework.

The two considerations behind direct investment in Europe are where to invest and how many plants to operate. The number of plants is

Figure 3.2 Matrix of economies of scale and distance

Economies of scale

		Low	High
	Low	peripheral	footloose
Distance costs	High	localized	central

dictated mostly by the potential for economies of scale in a particular industry. The decision on when to invest is a function of the costs of production in various locations together with the costs incurred in exporting from those locations. We refer to these latter costs as distance costs, i.e. the penalties imposed on an exporter by being far removed from the final market for its products. They are commonly assumed to relate to transportation costs, but they should be seen more broadly in terms of *marketing* costs, not in the sense of distribution and advertising, but rather all those elements, such as non-tradability, sophistication of the product, reliability, etc., that contribute to market-based FDI.

Figure 3.2 describes how firms will adopt different strategies depending on the strength of these two parameters. It is a well-known axiom that firms have several alternatives when it comes to organizing themselves internally and that the optimal hierarchical structure may evolve over time. Some firms have moved from a structure where affiliates in each country are miniature replicas of the parent to one where each affiliate specializes in a particular product market rather than a geographical one. The Single Market will hasten such a reorganization in many sectors, but it will not make it an inevitable structure for all firms. The food industry provides one example of where national tastes differ strongly within Europe, thus serving to keep the European market fragmented. Firms faced with this fragmentation will adopt 'localized' strategies. Distance costs in this case refer to the difficulties in penetrating markets dominated by strong national brands.

In other industries, the Single Market may represent opportunities for rationalized production. These industries fit into the other three boxes of Figure 3.2, depending on the importance of distance costs and economies of scale. When there are no obstacles to exporting throughout the Community, firms are virtually free to locate wherever they choose. Presumably, investors will reflect on the comparative advantage of each country and will invest where a country's specialization best matches their particular needs. Labour-intensive production might shift to the periphery while firms requiring skilled workers will look, for example, to Germany. In either case, the investor will also be influenced by government incentives.

Because every country has a comparative advantage in producing something, it is wrong to view a regional division of labour simply as a shift of production to the periphery. Nevertheless, labour is the least mobile factor of production and labour costs still differ widely within Europe, so investment in the periphery should be an important indication of this process at work. For this reason, we refer to firms adopting such a strategy as 'peripheral'.

'Footloose' firms are the Eurochampions envisaged by parts of the Commission. Once barriers to trade are removed, such firms will merge and serve the Single Market from fewer production bases. The choice of location for these firms is, in principle, flexible and difficult to determine *a priori*. With low distance costs, they may be tempted to shift to the periphery, but the often capital-intensive nature of their production will make wages of lesser importance in overall production costs. Such footloose firms are likely to be influenced by government incentives and the degree of regulation in each location.

Even if firms view Europe as a Single Market, they may still prefer to locate their activities close to the largest market for their products. Manufacturing hundreds or thousands of miles from the end-user or consumer may be perceived as a risky venture for a firm if flexibility, speed of delivery or some other competitive advantage of the company is deemed to be important. Typically, because the home market is the largest one, a firm will not shift its activities even when the market is enlarged. A recent study of the motor industry by Noble (1992, p. 119) suggested that Ford's reluctance to shift production from Britain to the continent in spite of higher productivity levels in the latter stems from the fact that 'the UK market represents the bulk of its car sales, mostly in the fleet market, where buyer power is high and margins are eroded. The company has national loyalty through long history there, and is unwilling to relocate because of market dependence.' Beyond a certain gap in productivity levels, this hesitation to relocate will disappear.

Not all firms in this category will necessarily remain at home. Those finding that a foreign market has become more important than the domestic one may well choose to relocate. Pilkington of the UK, the world's largest glass-maker, decided in 1991 to shift the headquarters of one of its core businesses to Brussels, acknowledging the 'difficulty of trying to run a £1.3 billion European business from the periphery of the single market.'[5] Other examples all come from American firms shifting some headquarters activities to Europe. Du Pont, Hewlett–Packard, IBM and Monsanto all transferred various divisions to Europe because the European market had become the largest one for the company or because it was expected to have the fastest growth in the 1990s. As a spokesman for Du Pont put it, Europe 'is where our main customers and main competitors are.'[6] Many of these firms were already producing in Europe, so the transfer of headquarters was simply a recognition that market proximity also eventually required managerial responsibility and that the largest market was the best place to manage global responsibilities for that product division.

Why would firms necessarily want to locate in the centre of the Single Market? As Krugman (1991, p. 96) explains,

> The reason is that reducing transportation costs has two effects: it facilitates locating production where it is cheapest, but it also facilitates concentration of production in one location, so as to realise economies of scale. And when production is concentrated, it may pay to concentrate it at the location with higher costs but better access.

This notion of better access is at the heart of what we call market-based FDI.

All four strategies described in Figure 3.2 can be found in Europe. Case-studies would provide insights into the nature of market fragmentation and the exact advantages to be derived from market proximity, as well as the role of labour costs and government incentives for particular firms. But they would not offer clues to which strategy is most prevalent at an aggregate level across the full spectrum of industries, including both manufacturing and services. One way to do this is to look at information provided on direct investment in Europe, though this approach also suffers from various shortcomings, not least the important question of what the statistics actually tell us. Nevertheless, it is possible to tease out a good deal of consistent though circumstantial evidence to suggest that market proximity is important for firms when choosing where to locate within Europe. This evidence is presented in the next chapter.

4

EUROPEAN INTEGRATION, TRADE AND INVESTMENT PATTERNS

The question of how Europe will evolve in the 1990s as the Single Market takes effect is a fundamental one. Particular attention has been focused on the effects on the periphery, with Bliss and De Macedo (1990) arguing that potential outcomes in terms of convergence or divergence may change radically with only slight alterations in the underlying assumptions. Trade and direct investment patterns provide some insights into this process at work.

In this chapter, we describe briefly how trade in Europe has evolved following the various phases of integration, but our main concern is with investment patterns. Where do firms from one member state invest in the rest of Europe? What does this tell us about the relative importance of each of the strategies described in Chapter 3? Where do American and Japanese firms choose to locate in Europe and to what extent do they appear to view the Community as a Single Market? Patterns of trade and investment suggest that Europe may be divided into a series of market clusters among countries that share a common border or language. Furthermore, national markets still matter even as the Commission breaks down barriers to trade that artificially segment markets.

Patterns of trade in Europe
During the first three postwar decades, trade was the principal mechanism by which economic integration occurred, and tariffs were the most important barrier to trade. The removal of internal tariffs on trade among the original six members of the Common Market, combined with the imposition of a common external tariff, had a profound effect on the

Figure 4.1 Exports to Germany, 1959–79 (as percentage of total exports)

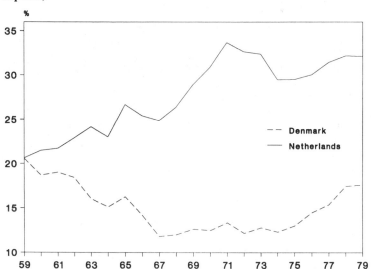

pattern of trade within Europe and hence on the degree to which the various economies became more integrated. Small European countries outside the preferential trading area of the Common Market were placed at a distinct disadvantage.

Figure 4.1 places in stark relief the contrasting trade effects on member and non-member countries. In the late 1950s, Denmark and Holland each sent roughly 20 per cent of their exports to Germany. Following the formation of the Common Market which included the Netherlands but not Denmark, the two shares moved sharply in opposite directions. By the early 1970s, the German market, was over twice as important to Dutch exporters as it was to Danish ones in relative terms. The Danish share recovered quickly in the 1970s after Denmark's accession to the Community in 1973. Although Danish exports to Germany continued to grow in absolute terms over the whole period, it is safe to say that as a result of the Common Market, the integration of the Dutch economy with the German one proceeded at a faster pace than was the case for Denmark.

In addition to tariffs, historical or cultural ties greatly affected trade patterns. It may seem strange today to think that Britain remained outside the Common Market until 1973, given that Germany, France and the Netherlands are now its largest export markets in Europe. In 1958, however, British trade with EFTA (including Denmark and Ireland) was only slightly less than its trade with the original six members of the Common Market.

The example of Danish exports to Germany shows that, in the 1960s, tariffs could still significantly influence trade and hence integration. The decision on whether to join the Community could have profound implications for the pattern of trade of a small European country. By the early 1970s the impact of tariff reductions had mostly exhausted itself and remaining non-tariff barriers proved more difficult to dislodge. Jacquemin and Sapir (1988, p. 131) look at intra-EC trade in manufactures for the older members of the Community and find that the intra-EC share of total EC imports grew steadily until the early 1970s but then remained at that level throughout the 1970s and fell back slightly in the 1980s. This declining share is seen as an indication that global integration has effectively caught up with European integration and that 'this apparent loss of competitiveness has recently prompted efforts towards freeing the internal market from enduring non-tariff barriers.'

After 35 years of gradual integration, the exports from individual countries to the rest of Europe are still highly concentrated in only a few markets, much more so than the relative market size of each importing country would suggest. The top three export markets within the Community for each member state take in between 56 and 77 per cent of total intra-EC exports from that country. Naturally the largest economies figure prominently in this list as export markets, but market proximity is also a factor. Balassa and Bauwens (1988) look at the determinants of the pattern of intra-European trade and find that market size, distance, common borders and similar languages are all more important than membership of the Community or EFTA in explaining both the importance of intra-industry trade and the pattern of overall trade in Europe.

Wijkman (1990) has taken the analysis of geographical factors further by looking at what he calls webs of dependency. He finds that there are three sub-regional trade blocs in Europe. The first is the North Periphery, consisting of the British Isles and Scandinavia. The second is the South Periphery, comprising the Iberian peninsula, Greece and Turkey. The remaining countries are clustered around Germany and called Core Europe. In comparing the trade pattern in 1958 with that in 1987, he finds that in many cases these clusters have become more, rather than less, clearly defined as a result of greater integration.

While trade patterns provide clues to the *process* of integration, the various types of trade tell us about the *nature* of that integration.

Greenaway (1987) has shown that European integration coincided not so much with greater inter-industry trade in Europe (as traditional trade theory would predict) as with intra-industry trade. This trend was not just limited to the members of the Common Market so it is far from clear that integration was the cause, but the rise of intra-industry trade clearly had an effect on the potential gains from integration. Krugman (1985, p. 41) has been instrumental in arguing that the gains from such trade stem from greater consumer choice and, more importantly, increased competition, rather than from increased inter-industry specialization. The importance of this argument with respect to direct investment in Europe will become clear later.

Patterns of investment in Europe

The history of FDI in Europe has been in many ways the obverse of trends in trade. While intra-EC trade was expanding rapidly in the 1960s, intra-European direct investment was negligible. The UK was the only important overseas investor and British firms were mostly interested in investing in Commonwealth countries and in the United States.

The United Nations Centre on Transnational Corporations (UNCTC 1991, p. 54) has documented the tendency for the three legs of what it calls the Triad (Europe, the US and Japan) to dominate investment flows within their respective regions. With the exception of Brazil, where German firms are abundant, Latin America is dominated by American MNEs. European MNEs are most active in Eastern Europe and in certain former colonies such as India. Japanese firms prevail within many of the fast-growing economies of East Asia. There are numerous exceptions, but the phenomenon of clustering clearly exists.

The same clustering exists within Europe. A good deal of the pattern of investment in Europe can be explained by the size of the host country market, together with some measure of proximity such as distance or a common language or border. In the Appendix we perform regressions with these variables to demonstrate their persistent significance in characterizing the pattern of intra-European investment. In this section, we rely on a more descriptive approach which seeks to delineate the various market clusters within western Europe.

The data provided on FDI in Europe are not sufficient to allow us to discuss the pattern of flows in any systematic way. Not only do definitions differ across countries, but the pattern itself is strongly distorted by the presence of holding companies located in Switzerland, the Nether-

47

Table 4.1 Direct investment in Europe from selected countries (% of total investment in Europe for each country)

Country of Investment	Investor									
	US	J	F	D	I	NL	UK	S	DK	E
EC12	85	94	88	83	83	80	78	80	82	92
Belg.–Lux.	5	3	17	11	2	21	6	na	3	13
Denmark	1	0	1	1	0	1	2	8	–	0
France	8	7	–	16	12	13	18	6	15	11
Germany	14	8	8	–	10	17	13	8	12	8
Greece	0	0	0	1	0	1	0	na	0	0
Ireland	3	1	0	4	0	1	6	na	6	0
Italy	6	2	8	9	–	2	7	na	0	5
Luxembourg	1	10	*	6	23	*	*	na	*	*
Netherlands	11	22	27	11	17	–	21	26	15	14
Portugal	0	0	1	1	0	0	3	na	0	19
Spain	4	3	12	10	8	5	11	1	4	–
UK	32	39	13	13	11	16	–	15	24	21
EFTA	15	6	12	17	17	22	12	20	18	8
Austria	0	0	0	6	0	na	1	0	0	0
Finland	0	0	0	0	0	na	0	4	0	0
Norway	2	1	0	1	0	na	2	7	4	0
Sweden	1	0	0	1	0	na	2	–	11	0
Switzerland	12	4	12	8	17	na	6	10	4	8
EUROPE	100	100	100	100	100	100	100	100	100	100
TOTAL (bn ecus)	135.8	43.4	33.5	51.3	32.5	36.0	39.2	22.2	4.6	1.2

Note: US, Japan (J), Germany (D), Italy (I), Netherlands (NL), UK, Sweden (S): stock figures, 1990; France (F): stock figure, 1989; Denmark (DK), Spain (E): cumulative flows. *Luxembourg figure is included in Belgium.

lands and Luxembourg. If the description that follows appears selective, it is because of these shortcomings in the data and not because of our wish to tell only one side of the story.

Table 4.1 shows the pattern and level of intra-European investments from the most important home countries, with US and Japanese patterns in Europe added for comparison. Any comparison of the different levels of outward investment from each country must be made cautiously. Not only are some figures more recent than others, but some refer to stocks while others are based on cumulative flows. Even the definition of what constitutes FDI differs greatly across countries, with some countries such as the US, the UK and Germany including retained earnings while others such as Japan, France and Spain exclude them. The importance of retained earnings depends very much on the age of the investment. For American investment in Europe, virtually all of the increase over the past 20 years has come about from retained earnings. If they had not been included in the total then we would have seen no new investment in Europe from America over the period. For more recent investors, retained earnings contribute only a small share of total flows, but the rapid growth of Japanese investment means that this bias will soon loom larger.

Keeping in mind these various caveats, the levels of investment in Europe in Table 4.1 show first that the US is by far the largest investor in Europe, while the four largest EC countries, together with the Netherlands and Japan, are all in the range of 30–50 billion ecus. Any precise ranking of the countries would be misleading in view of the earlier discussion. Nevertheless, it is safe to say that in terms of intra-EC flows, no country appears as an outlier. Britain may dominate extra-EC flows, but it is only one of many investors within Europe. More can be deduced by looking at where firms from each country have invested in the rest of Europe.

Britain is the preferred choice of American and Japanese firms by a wide margin, with almost twice as much inward investment as the next nearest host country, but it does not loom disproportionately large as a host to intra-European flows. In contrast, Germany appears to be slightly under-represented as a host country. While at first glance this would seem to confirm that Germany is both a difficult market to enter and an expensive place to produce, the evidence is not so compelling if we look only at manufacturing. In terms of employment, Germany ranks second behind the UK and ahead of France for Japanese and US manufacturing firms. Furthermore, the German share of American manufacturing investment has been growing quickly and may well have overtaken the UK in 1992. Recent American investment in eastern Germany has no doubt added to this trend. Germany is also among the favoured locations in Europe for Dutch and British firms. These figures lend little support to the notion that firms are shying away from producing in Germany.

The consistent importance of Switzerland, Luxembourg or the Netherlands in the overall figures may result in large part from the role that those countries play as hosts to holding companies or financial affiliates of firms from other EC countries. Italian investment, born out of the need to circumvent capital controls, is the prime example of this phenomenon. Fully 57 per cent of its outward European investment goes to those three countries. Similarly, Luxembourg attracts a disproportionate share of the

Table 4.2 Intra-European direct investment into selected countries (% of total inward investment from Europe for each country)

Investor	D	UK	NL	I	F	E	DK	S	B–L	IRL
				Host country						
EC12	63	76	71	66	77	88	36	47	87	87
Belg. – Lux.	4	4	18	10	11	5	5	5	–	3
France	12	18	8	18	–	22	10	2	31	9
Germany	–	12	14	10	16	12	9	7	17	28
Italy	5	2	0	–	10	5	0	0	2	1
Netherlands	24	37	–	14	18	29	8	13	19	7
UK	15	–	28	14	21	14	5	10	17	37
Other EC	3	4	2	0	1	2	0	10	2	2
EFTA	37	24	29	34	23	11	64	53	13	13
Austria	3	0	na	0	0	0	0	0	na	1
Finland	1	1	na	0	1	0	4	15	na	1
Norway	0	2	na	0	1	0	19	12	na	1
Sweden	9	8	na	4	10	2	43	–	na	6
Switzerland	24	14	18	30	10	10	0	27	na	4
EUROPE	100	100	100	100	100	100	100	100	100	100
TOTAL (bn ecus)	38.2	59.4	31.1	34.9	36.2	43.9	4.4	7.8	15.9	na

Note: Germany (D), UK, Netherlands (NL), Italy (I), Sweden (S): stock figures for 1990; France (F), Spain (E), Denmark (DK), Belgium–Luxembourg (B–L): cumulative flows; Ireland (IRL): manufacturing employment.

European investments of Japanese and German banks. These investments are clearly driven by differences in regulations across Europe, much as American firms prefer to be incorporated in Delaware, where certain regulations are more favourable than in other states. Such investment has little to do with direct investment in the traditional sense but rather represents the transfer, on paper at least, of portfolio capital through the affiliate for use elsewhere, possibly even back in the home country.

Even disregarding financial affiliates, outward investment in Europe is often concentrated in only a few countries. The first choice for individual countries often attracts well over 20 per cent of total flows. Anywhere from 29 to 45 per cent of intra-European investments by German, French, British and Dutch firms go to only two countries. Investment into Europe from outside the Community is even more concentrated.

Table 4.2 looks at intra-EC flows from the perspective of the host country. The same caveats apply as for outflows with regard to both the absolute levels and the pattern. With the exception of the UK, the major countries (including Spain this time) are within the range of 30–50 billion ecus. The Spanish figure is biased upward by the fact that it relates to notifications rather than actual investment. Given that Britain did not appear as an outlier in Table 4.1 when we looked at where other member states invested in Europe, why does the UK appear so prominent as a host country on the basis of its own statistics? The answer is quite simply that Dutch investments in the UK alone amount to 22 billion ecus which is more than many other small countries invest in the whole of Europe. This investment is in turn dominated by the oil sector and indicates how much binational companies can affect the FDI figures. If we were to remove Royal Dutch/Shell from the total figures, the UK would probably more closely resemble other member states.

The pattern of inflows is even more distorted by holding companies and finance affiliates than were outflows. The Netherlands and Switzerland account for 61 per cent of British inflows from Europe, and between 39 and 48 per cent of European investment in Spain, Italy and Germany. If we look only at the relationship between the four largest countries (EC4) and the periphery, one country often prevails over the other three in particular host countries. British firms account for 37 per cent of employment by European firms in Ireland. The case of investment in Ireland is described in more detail in Box 4.1. French firms represent 45 per cent of EC4 investment in Belgium–Luxembourg and 42 per cent in Spain. In other cases, the principal investors are not the EC4 or Switzerland and the Netherlands but rather neighbouring countries. Almost two-thirds of European investment into Denmark comes from Sweden and Norway.

The role of geographical and cultural proximity is confirmed if we look once again from the home country perspective in Table 4.1. German firms dominate EC4 investments in Austria, employing more Austrians than they do Spaniards or even British and more Swiss than Greeks and Portuguese combined. Denmark has invested three times as much in Sweden since 1978 as it has in Belgium, an economy of roughly similar size. Almost two-thirds of German investment in western Europe goes to the seven countries that border on that country, while much of the rest goes to the three remaining large markets of Britain, Spain and Italy. Dutch firms invest the most in Belgium–Luxembourg. Spanish firms prefer Portugal and then France.

Box 4.1 Ireland

Ireland is a small country on the periphery of Europe. It has the second smallest market within the Community after Luxembourg, and the Irish Sea has been referred to as 'one of the most expensive stretches of water in the world'.[1] In spite of these handicaps, Ireland has succeeded in enticing investors and, as a result, has a higher penetration of foreign firms relative to the size of its market than virtually all other OECD countries except for Canada.

Partly through EC membership, Ireland has managed to shift away from its complete dependence on the UK as an export market, down from 92 per cent of total Irish intra-Community exports to 44 per cent in 1991. Foreign-owned firms have no doubt contributed to this process: the evidence suggests that American MNEs export three-quarters of their Irish output. Overall, foreign-owned firms account for 80 per cent of Irish manufactured exports.

Fully one-half of this investment is from American MNEs. American investment grew most quickly after 1973, when Ireland joined the EC along with the UK and Denmark. American, Japanese and Korean firms accounted for over 100 per cent of the net increase in jobs in foreign-owned firms between 1987 and the end of 1991. If Ireland is an export platform for the British Isles and for Europe as a whole, it is non-EC firms that are benefiting the most from it. In a recent study of Taiwanese and Korean investment in Europe, McDermott (1992) suggests that the choice of Ireland by firms from these countries represents a compromise between market proximity and staying at home. These firms recognize the importance of market proximity to enhance their brand image and to gather information about local demand and technologies, but at the same time they cannot quite compete head on with the major players on the basis of anything but wage costs.

In contrast to the continued growth of non-EC investments, manufacturing employment in EC-owned MNEs in Ireland has actually fallen since 1987. Within the overall Community figures, only Germany has managed to increase its employment substantially over the period, which suggests that German firms may be looking for lower-wage countries outside their own country.

What emerges for both inflows and outflows is the importance of market size and geographical proximity in shaping the pattern of investment within Europe. With the exception of certain financial centres, the flow of virtually all intra-European direct investment is either to the largest countries or to those located near to the investor. Given that proximity appears again and again, can we identify any potential clusters within Europe for investment, as was the case for trade? If we take the UNCTC's measure of relative dominance, in which one European investor must hold 10 per cent more of the total stock than the next country, then how

Whether German production in Ireland constitutes a regional division of labour depends on the market it is intended to serve. Output from German plants in Ireland may be destined, first and foremost, for the British market. The available statistics do not provide any clues.

Irish government policies towards inward investment
To attract firms, the Irish government offers a 10 per cent corporate tax rate until the year 2000 for most companies, no restrictions on repatriation of profits, and various other loans and grants, e.g. for training. In part a result of selective targeting, the industrial composition of foreign-owned firms is heavily concentrated in high-technology, capital-intensive sectors. According to the OECD (1985), the result in a country with abundant labour is

> the emergence of a dual industrial economy. On the one hand, foreign firms have expanded output and exports rapidly and enjoy very high levels of productivity. On the other hand, the indigenous sector has only recently halted its rapid decline in domestic market share, and productivity levels are low despite recent improvements. Moreover, foreign-owned firms have developed few linkages with the indigenous economy, little in the way of local research or technological inputs, and depend heavily on imported raw materials and components ... Furthermore, there are considerable financial costs in attracting and maintaining foreign investment, and the 10 per cent manufacturing corporation profits tax has provided little direct corporate revenue for the Exchequer.

Nor has the employment of almost 100,000 Irish workers made much of a dent in the level of unemployment, which remains one of the highest in Europe. Of course, it is not possible to say whether unemployment would have been higher in the absence of inward investment. These criticisms of Irish policies have led to a rethink within the Irish government towards a more balanced approach that attempts more explicitly to foster indigenous industry.

many actual clusters can be identified? Unfortunately, there is always going to be the problem that part of this investment is channelled through holding companies or financial affiliates in one of the European offshore centres. In what follows we will mostly disregard the Netherlands and Switzerland. We must also remember that this discussion relates to intra-European investment. In many cases, the principal investors are American MNEs

Austria is clearly within Germany's economic sphere, as the bordering Eastern European states may well find themselves in the future. Inward investment in Spain and Belgium–Luxembourg is dominated by firms

Box 4.2 Portugal

Portugal joined the Community in 1986. This resulted in a massive inflow of investment, with inflows doubling every year between 1987 and 1989. Britain, France and Spain are the major European investors, with only 7–8 per cent of recent flows coming from the US. Investments by American firms, however, undoubtedly loom much larger in the Portuguese economy than these figures suggest. Three of the largest manufacturing investments have involved Ford and General Motors, for example. This is a good indication of the problems in trying to distinguish between what is recorded for balance-of-payments purposes and the exact origin of the investing firm. The balance of payments is concerned with the geographical origin or destination of a particular capital flow, not who owns that capital. Thus, if Ford invested in Portugal through its affiliate in the UK, it would be recorded as a British investment. Brazil accounts for roughly five per cent of total inflows, which suggests the importance of cultural and linguistic links, just as Mexican firms have been known to invest in Spain as a gateway to Europe.

By sector, two-thirds of inflows have been in the service sector: finance, insurance, real estate, trades and hotels. Service firms are attracted by the increased growth prospects and stability that EC membership allows, as well as the removal of various capital controls and the privatization and deregulation of many sectors such as in banking. Manufacturing represents only one-quarter of total inflows. In a sample of manufacturing investments, Simões (1992, p. 12) found that, in value terms, almost two-thirds of the manufacturers were primarily export-oriented while the remaining investments were market-based. This export emphasis was mostly due to two very large investments in the automotive sector. Ford invested to produce car radios while General Motors–Delco began producing ignition systems. Since then, Ford and Volkswagen of Germany have established a joint venture to produce multipurpose vehicles, Valmet of Finland plans to build tractors and Continental of Germany has agreed to a joint venture to produce tyres.

At $3.1 billion, the Ford–VW joint venture far exceeds the four other major manufacturing investments mentioned above, which together amount to about $250 million. It will employ 5,000 Portuguese directly, with perhaps twice that number employed in support industries. Exports from the joint venture

from neighbouring France. Ireland is host to more British firms than to any other group, though German firms have slowly eaten away at the British monopoly. The Netherlands is firmly tied to the UK, and Denmark is a host primarily to other Scandinavian firms. British firms also prevail in Portugal owing to historical commercial links between those two countries (initially in part for the export of port wine), while Spanish outflows are heavily concentrated on the Portuguese market (see Box 4.2).

will account for 25–30 per cent of total Portuguese exports and presumably a high share of imports as well. Why did such a large investment come to Portugal? One possibility is lower wages. Several investors have commented in *The Financial Times* that productivity levels are not substantially different from those elsewhere,[2] corroborating the evidence from the MIT survey (Womack et al. 1990) mentioned in Chapter 3. If this is true, then Portuguese wages are a significant inducement for some firms in spite of the lower average productivity in Portugal. But, as one investor pointed out in relation to the Ford–VW venture, 'low wages have to be put in perspective, this is a capital-intensive project'.[3]

The other inducement is undoubtedly investment incentives, amounting to Es120 billion out of the total Es450 billion Ford–VW venture. Of the total incentive package, Es90 billion was a cash subsidy, 70 per cent of which was paid by the EC through its structural funds. The rest went to training subsidies and fiscal concessions, including a five-year tax exemption. Although there was fierce competition from other locations such as eastern Germany – which attracted an Opel (GM) plant – and Spain, it is hard to see how EC inducements tipped the balance in favour of Portugal since these same inducements were on offer at the other locations as well. Nevertheless, they may have compensated for any desire to remain closer to the core market in Europe.

These large-scale investments will have a major impact on the Portuguese economy and appear to correspond to a regional division of labour in Europe. The fact that they are almost all in the motor industry should not surprise us since, as we suggested in Chapter 3, it is the sector most likely to think regionally. But it is also important to keep in mind that they represent just a handful of the investments in Portugal, which totalled 3,500 projects in 1990 alone. Even in value terms, service sector firms still invest twice as much. The vast majority of investments in Portugal are to serve the local or Iberian market. To look only at the largest investments, however important they may be, is inappropriate. The other 3,498 investors that did not make the headlines in 1990 are far more important not only in value terms but also in terms of their effect on the economy by bringing capital, skills, technology and, potentially, competition to all parts of the economy.

These various links by and large conform to the patterns of trade described by Wijkman (1990). They confirm the dictum of John Kay (1990, p. 10) that '[it] is increasingly common for a merger to cross one European border, but it is still much less common for a merger to cross two.'

Although we have looked at clusters in terms of the relationship between peripheral countries and the large economies at the core of the Community, we do not necessarily mean to imply that within clusters there is purely a one-way flow from the core to the periphery. The same countries that rank highly for one member state's outflows are also likely to be important sources of inward investment for that state. Three of the top four host countries for German direct investment in Europe are also among the top four European investors in Germany. For French investment, seven out of eight major host countries are also the top home countries for European investment in France. For Britain, the three countries that take the lion's share of UK FDI in Europe also hold a virtual monopoly on European investment into Britain. The same is true if one looks only at manufacturing. For the Netherlands, six countries take 88 per cent of Dutch outflows to Europe and contribute 97 per cent of inflows.

The fact that so much investment follows the dictates of geography tells us little about the motive. It is quite conceivable that firms are seeking lower wages or a more favourable regulatory environment next door in one industry while a reverse flow is occurring in another sector. As long as policies and wages are sectorally differentiated, it is perfectly consistent to see such cross-hauling of investment. This argument becomes less tenable, however, when one considers that a fairly high proportion of intra-European flows is also intra-industry. For example, Unilever might invest in Switzerland at the same time as Nestlé establishes or acquires an affiliate in Britain.

It is difficult to pinpoint this behaviour in practice for the simple reason that the level of disaggregation at the sectoral level provided by national authorities is poor. Furthermore, when investments are made through holding companies, as with 38 per cent of German inflows, it is impossible to determine the exact industry of the investor. Nevertheless, certain evidence of intra-industry flows in Europe does emerge. Table 4.3 provides evidence of substantial intra-industry investment within the EC involving both the UK and Germany.

Intra-industry direct investment (IIDI) is difficult to reconcile with any notion that firms are investing abroad to take advantage of more favourable conditions for production in that country. We naturally cannot prove from this that such investment is not merely for the purposes of restructuring alone, since restructuring would also presumably be affected by distance. Nevertheless, the consistent importance of market size suggests that IIDI, like intra-industry trade, is a form of oligopolistic competition. Graham (1978) has shown that when firms from one country invest abroad, rivals in the host country are likely to respond by setting up affiliates in the other market. The extent to which such oligopolistic

Table 4.3 The index of intra-industry direct investment between the UK and the EC and Germany and the EC, 1987

Industry	UK	Germany
Food, drink and tobacco	0.31	0.92
Chemicals and allied	0.57	0.48
Metals	0.16	0.77
Mechanical engineering	0.92	0.60
Electrical equipment	0.83	0.83
Office equipment	na	0.47
Transport equipment	0.87	0.33
Paper and allied	0.12	na
Rubber	na	0.78
Non-metallic mineral products	na	0.65
Coal and petroleum products	na	0.03
Precision instruments	na	0.62
Other manufacturing	0.33	0.49
Total	0.47	0.74
Mean	0.47	0.53

Source: Adapted from Cantwell and Sanna Randaccio (1992).
Note: The index of intra-industry direct investment (IIDI) is given by:
$$IID_i = [(O_i+I_i) - (O_i - I_i)]$$
where O_i = outward DI stock in industry i
I_i = inward DI stock in industry i

rivalry reduces or heightens competition in the host country will be discussed in Chapter 6.

Conclusion

Through the welter of statistics on intra-European direct investment, several points emerge. The first is that the pattern of inflows for a European country often mirrors that of its outflows, both in distribution and in behaviour over time. Furthermore, much of this investment flows back and forth within the same industry. Removing barriers to trade and investment alters the pattern of flows, leading to greater integration. We have seen how Danish firms lost market share in Germany by remaining outside the Common Market. Spain and Portugal attracted tremendous inflows of direct investment in the late 1980s as a result of their accession to the Community. Eastern Europe will probably receive more of both trade and investment, particularly from Germany, following its opening up to the West, though the problems of adjustment will probably keep both at bay for a while. In all cases, policy shifts have dramatically affected trade and investment patterns in Europe. Once the dust has settled, however, patterns of exchange within Europe have tended to follow certain paths. Neither trade nor investment patterns suggest that the Single Market is a single market. A German firm is seven times more likely to export to Belgium than it is to Greece, two countries with similar population levels (though naturally differences in income levels also affect this tendency). The same German firm is also 17 times more likely to invest in Belgium than in Greece. There are cases of mergers that break free of geography, such as that between Volvo of Sweden and Renault of France, but they are the exception and not the rule.

The bulk of intra-European investment does not appear to represent a net transfer of resources to benefit from the comparative advantage of each country. As with trade flows, FDI in Europe appears to conform to the notion of a market subdivided into clusters, with much trade and investment flowing both ways within the same industry. It is possible to argue that what we are observing is some form of hysteresis in which existing patterns are the result of previous policies and that the Single Market has yet to manifest itself in investment patterns, but evidence from previous phases of integration presented below suggests that trade barriers are not the only cause of this segmentation.

To get a better sense of whether investment patterns in Europe are evolving in the direction of a regional division of labour, we now turn to Japanese and American investments in Europe. American investment presents a long and consistent historical record from which we can assess the whole period of European integration. The US Commerce Department also provides more information on the activities of American firms in Europe than do European governments on their own firms. If US MNE behaviour gives us a long historical record, Japanese investment provides a glimpse of the most important influences on the location of investment today. Many Japanese firms intend to serve the whole market and almost all are offered inducements from host governments. We shall discuss these inducements in the next chapter.

American direct investment in Europe

When American firms first began to invest in Europe in the middle of the nineteenth century, their natural preference was to locate in Britain, the richest market in the world at the time. The greatest push into Europe came in the 1960s and 1970s; since then, although many large investments have been made, most of the addition to the stock of American investment in Europe has come through retained earnings of existing affiliates. It is generally agreed that these US MNEs, with their long history in Europe and their experience in serving a large market at home, are among the most pan-European of firms. As such, their location decisions should best reflect their appraisal of the comparative advantage of each European country.

The distribution of American investment in Europe was shown in Table 4.1. Britain is not only first overall, but also first in many individual industries. Britain's role in the oil sector may be understandable given that it is an oil exporter, just as the importance of London as an international financial centre helps to explain its role in services, but why in manufacturing as well? The fact that Britain ranks first in food, chemicals and electronics as well as second in metals and transport equipment flies in the face of comparative advantage. It simply cannot be the best place to produce everything.

In trying to explain why Britain has been the first choice of American firms in Europe, it is difficult to separate the fact that the common use of English presents less of a barrier to US MNEs from the historical importance of the large UK market. Over time, the British share has fallen as both its relative size has shrunk and the cultural distance between America and the rest of Europe has diminished for US MNEs after decades of operating on a pan-European basis. But it is vital to keep in mind that the British share has not fallen steadily and has indeed managed to represent a fairly constant one-third of the European total for US FDI since Britain joined the EC in 1973. One reason may simply be that its market size continues to draw in US firms even as other attractions fade.

Throughout our discussion, we take the size of each national market as the appropriate variable in influencing investment. Another possibility is that the relevant market for a firm investing for the first time is the market share of the investor that has been achieved through exports. The notion that exports can encourage FDI by reducing the information costs involved when penetrating foreign markets is not a controversial one. By offering a relatively open market for American goods, Britain may have attracted a larger share of the investment by American MNEs in Europe.

Table 4.4 compares the pattern of investment and trade for the US and Japan with Europe. For American firms, at least, the pattern of trade closely mirrors that of investment. The explanation for this correlation is open to debate. Both trade and investment may be driven by a common

Table 4.4 Distribution of Japanese and US exports and FDI (% of each country in EC total)

Country	Japan		US	
	FDI	Exports	FDI	Exports
UK	36	19	24	23
Netherlands	22	12	9	10
Germany	12	32	23	21
France	11	11	14	18
Spain	9	6	6	6
Belg.–Lux.	5	7	6	7
Italy	3	7	10	9
Ireland	1	1	6	3
Denmark	0	2	0	2
Greece	0	2	0	1
Portugal	1	1	1	1

Source: Adapted from Thomsen and Nicolaides (1991).

set of factors, or exports may precede investment as in the product cycle. To make the matter more complex, a good many American exports to Europe are now transferred between US firms and their European affiliates. Nevertheless, even if we compare current investment patterns with trade patterns in previous decades, the relationship is still a strong one, which suggests that intra-firm trade is not behind this correlation. For whatever reason, there is a close relationship between where America exports in Europe and where American firms choose to invest. The Japanese case will be discussed later.

The advantage of looking at American investment is that it gives us not only a long historical perspective but also a glimpse of the behaviour of US-owned firms within Europe. Sales patterns of American firms in Europe tell us about the extent to which the region is viewed as a single market by American firms. A truly integrated market would allow subsidiaries to supply the whole of Europe from a particular location. For many industries, such is not the case.

American manufacturing subsidiaries in Europe sell 60 per cent of their output in the national market in which they are located. This share has fallen over time, as one would expect given the increasing degree of integration, but since 1977 it has remained largely unchanged for all 12 countries combined. Some countries such as Spain and Portugal have seen the local share fall precipitously since 1977, just as occurred for

Table 4.5 Sales by US manufacturing affiliates in Europe and percentages sold locally

Country	1977		1989	
	US$m	%	US$m	%
Belgium	2,035	29	4,932	30
Denmark	241	51	662	57
France	10,798	68	23,546	67
Germany	19,042	65	41,060	57
Greece	270	79	430	84
Ireland	229	20	2,282	25
Italy	5,020	73	17,300	73
Luxembourg	45	11	304	28
Netherlands	2,842	39	7,431	33
Portugal	314	91	723	57
Spain	3,334	81	12,533	70
UK	18,261	69	57,364	72
EC12	62,432	62	168,567	60

Source: US Department of Commerce.

some of the smaller member states in earlier decades. But for most of the other EC countries excluding the new members, the local share of sales has actually risen over the past 15 years. These shares are presented in Table 4.5 and suggest that integration does have an effect on the behaviour of MNEs, particularly in its early phases. But there appear to be limits to the degree to which firms will treat Europe as one market, and for larger countries this limit may already have been reached.

Extrapolating on the basis of past trends is risky given that the Single Market may change firms' perceptions as previous phases of integration could not. But if we look carefully at which countries export more and at the pattern of exports from those countries, we can see that the behaviour of firms is still conditioned by market proximity.

The distribution of sales tells only part of the story. Exports may be a high percentage of total sales from some countries but subsidiaries in the largest markets are still the greatest exporters. Germany, the least likely location for export-oriented investment in terms of labour costs and environmental regulations, accounts for 30 per cent of total intra-EC exports of American firms. Britain and France together contribute another 28 per cent. Much of the rest comes from Benelux and Ireland. The appeal of these smaller countries stems from their location next to the largest national markets for American firms' goods. Investment in Ben-

Table 4.6 Sales by US affiliates in Europe by industry, 1989

Industry	I (US$m)	II (US$m)	Ratio I/II
Total	380,090	162,806	2.3
Oil	70,520	14,125	5.0
Manufacturing:	173,830	98,658	1.8
Food	22,171	7,320	3.0
Chemicals	34,450	24,207	1.4
Metals	6,755	3,994	1.7
Machinery	33,878	19,290	1.8
Electronics	9,389	5,148	1.8
Transportation equipment	30,950	23,444	1.3
Other	36,237	15,256	2.4
Wholesale	95,211	40,699	2.3
Finance, insurance, property	15,409	1,954	7.9
Services	15,892	6,145	2.6
Other	9,226	1,224	7.5

Source: US Department of Commerce
I Local sales by affiliates in the national markets in which they are located.
II Exports by affiliates (except those to the US).

elux and Ireland is both market-based, in the sense of being drawn to the German and British markets, and factor-based, in that these countries offer lower costs than Britain and Germany. Nevertheless, US firms still prefer to sell locally in the largest markets rather than exporting from neighbouring countries.

Unfortunately, we possess little information about where within Europe these affiliates sell when they export. The most recent information comes from a 1977 survey by the US Commerce Department. It found that affiliate exports in Belgium were fairly widely dispersed given the central location of that country within Europe. Nevertheless, many of the exports went to Germany, France and the Netherlands, in that order. Affiliates in Ireland were found to export primarily to the UK while those in Denmark focused on Sweden and Germany. Affiliates in the largest markets predominantly exported among themselves, though neighbouring countries were also targeted. Indeed, the main conclusion that emerges from these export patterns is that the behaviour of American firms in Europe is not much different from that of local firms. In almost all cases, the top four markets for affiliate exports within Europe were also the same as for total host country exports, though the exact ranking was often slightly different. This suggests that clustering is as much a phenomenon for US affiliate exports as it is for the total pattern of intra-European trade as described by Wijkman (1990).

US FDI statistics also allow us to see the extent to which our conclusions are industry-specific. Table 4.6 compares local sales with exports (excluding exports to the US) for American firms in Europe by industry. As one might expect, services are most likely to be sold locally, but even in manufacturing all major industries sell more in the national market than in the European one. The exact ratio varies between three times as much sold locally by food companies and 1.3 times as much for the transportation equipment industries. These are the two industries that we have used as our extreme cases in previous discussions. Table 4.6 suggests that the extremes are not that far apart. Indeed, what is surprising is how consistent the share of local sales to exports appears to be across industries.

The American investment experience in Europe thus provides several insights into MNE behaviour. US MNEs tend to invest in or near their largest markets and to sell mostly in those markets. Affiliates in the Benelux countries may export a large share of what they produce, but it is still much less than affiliates in Britain and Germany. And exports to the Community are on the whole much less important than local sales. The tale is one of firms driven by the need to be close to their most important markets. We cannot tell whether the significance of market size for American firms means that they are 'localized' or 'central', but the mere fact that so much of what affiliates produce is sold in the national market in which they are located suggests strongly that they are following a 'localized' strategy.

Japanese direct investment in Europe

While American investment provides clues to long-term trends, Japanese investment is fairly recent and often occurs through greenfield plants rather than acquisitions. It thus reflects quite well the current perception of the competing attractions of various locations within Europe. Given their virtual freedom of action, it is surprising how much Japanese firms' location choices mirror those of US MNEs across a wide range of industries. Britain is once again heavily favoured.

In an econometric test, Yamawaki (1991) identifies some of the most significant influences on the distribution of Japanese FDI within Europe. He finds that location strategies broadly reflect the comparative advantage of each host country. Japanese firms prefer countries with lower wages in spite of the inferior levels of productivity in those countries. In high technology sectors, they prefer countries with indigenous technological capabilities. In keeping with the findings of virtually all such tests on direct investment, Yamawaki finds that the size of the national market in which the firm locates is also an important consideration. Since the significance of national market size is inconsistent with the view that the Single Market is the relevant one for Japanese MNEs, he suggests that the Single Market is an expectation rather than an actuality.

Thomsen and Nicolaides (1991) suggest that one reason why Japanese manufacturers prefer Britain which is often given insufficient attention is the fact that it has traditionally been such a large market for Japanese exports. Britain was the largest market for Nissan when it invested, for example, and for many products such as microwave ovens in the 1970s before Japanese investment in those sectors. Britain also far exceeds other markets in Europe in terms of its purchases of video-cassette recorders (VCRs). Similarly, although Japanese motor industry investment in Spain is seen as part of a regional strategy on the part of Nissan and Toyota, much of this investment dates from the 1970s when poor-quality but low-priced car exports from Japan were more suited to the closed and uncompetitive Spanish market than they were to the rest of the EC. Nevertheless, these plants are becoming more integrated with the rest of the Community over time.

Table 4.4 compares total Japanese exports with manufacturing investment in Europe by country. The relationship between the two is by no means as close as it was for American firms. In particular, Germany is the largest export market but Britain receives the most investment. This merely serves to highlight the fact that market size, whether measured by GNP or exports, is only one of the factors behind the location decision. Germany is an expensive place to produce and its firms are often highly competitive; both of these factors may have served to discourage Japanese investors. Nevertheless, by other measures of Japanese manufacturing involvement such as employment levels or number of affiliates, Germany figures much more prominently, though still behind the UK.

On the basis of surveys of Japanese investors, Hood and Truijens (1992, p. 9) suggest how the relationship between export markets and investment choices may work in practice:

Firstly, and at the root of the whole matter, is the question of market size. The presence of sales offices in the large country markets, namely France, Germany, and the UK, invariably means that they are part of the consideration [of where to invest]. They do not, however, have equal weight in that France is usually developed later and these offices often report through German or UK routes to Japan. Among other factors, this places France at a disadvantage in locational competition.

It is interesting to compare Japanese location decisions in Europe with similar ones in the more integrated US market. Looking at Japanese manufacturing start-ups in the United States, Woodward (1992) finds that market size (with a control variable to normalize for the fact that larger geographical areas are more likely to attract more firms) is consistently the most significant factor explaining where Japanese firms choose to locate factories. Market size in this case is not just defined as the state market but also includes the state's position relative to other state markets. Glickman and Woodward (1989) argue that foreign manufacturers are serving regional markets in the United States.

Woodward also looks at county-level location decisions once the state has been chosen. Once again, manufacturing agglomeration and population density appeal to Japanese investors. High productivity appears to be more important than low wages. Evidence from Japanese FDI in Europe suggests that firms may choose a depressed region in a fairly centrally located country but in a peripheral country proximity to the centre of the EC may matter more. According to Kume and Totsuke (1991, p. 46), 'Japanese companies seem to have set up relatively many factories in the assisted areas in the UK and in equivalent areas in France where investors are eligible for governmental aid.' In Spain, however, Thomsen and Nicolaides (1991, p. 32) point out that 'more that one half of Japanese companies ... are located in Catalonia which does not offer financial or fiscal incentives to industrial investors, whereas subsidies of up to 70 per cent of the investment are available in depressed areas.'

These disparate findings confirm that markets matter even for greenfield investment and that this tendency characterizes Japanese investment in both the United States and Europe. It is not necessarily the degree of integration that makes national markets important. Indeed, it is probably not the national market at all but rather market clustering that matters most and this may well spill over several markets. Firms congregate in areas of high or growing market demand.

Conclusion
What do the patterns of investment described in this chapter tell us about the possible motives behind firms' behaviour? The consistent importance of market size and proximity in shaping patterns of direct investment in Europe suggests (see Figure 3.2) that much of European industry can be classified as 'localized' or 'central' where distance costs play a major role in location decisions. Even if Japanese automobile producers are planning to serve the whole European market from their factories in England, the fact that they chose the UK in the first place may suggest that they may be 'central' rather than 'footloose'. Proximity to one of the largest national markets and to the core of the European market where the greatest concentration of consumers is located may still matter even if Europe is completely integrated. This conclusion also emerges from analysis of where Japanese firms have located in the United States.

In other sectors where economies of scale are less pronounced, the fact that markets matter may relate to the fragmented nature of demand in Europe, with goods and services differentiated across borders. Any sector where national brands are dominant could potentially drive firms to follow a strategy of localization. Markets matter in this case because they are different from one another.

Distance costs do not necessarily imply that firms are restricted to any geographical area. But if they do venture farther afield, then market size must be sufficiently large or unit labour costs sufficiently low to compensate for greater distances. These distance costs do not relate solely to physical distances. In terms of culture, Britain may still be closer to North America than to the Mediterranean, which may explain why bilateral investments between the US and the UK, at $174 billion, are the greatest between any two countries by a wide margin. This transatlantic love affair goes back a long way.

We cannot accurately assess the extent to which investment in the periphery is intended as an export platform solely from the FDI figures provided in this chapter. We can only state that the smaller peripheral countries (Ireland, Greece and Portugal) accounted for only three per cent of total EC inflows in 1991. Investment in Portugal is, however, growing quickly, and a case-study of motor industry investment in Portugal would have testified to the process of a regional division of labour at work in Europe. It would not have shown that total manufacturing investment in Portugal represents less than 0.5 per cent of total Community flows. These inflows may be very important for the countries concerned, but they have contributed little to the flourishing cross-border activities of

European firms in the 1980s and early 1990s, most of which has remained within the core countries. Firms with high labour requirements, where exporting over long distances is not an obstacle, have no reason necessarily to prefer a regional division of labour over a global one. Already many EC companies have more investment in tiny Singapore than they do in Portugal.

The prevalence of market clusters within Europe alters the notion of the periphery in Europe. Ireland may be on the periphery of Europe but it is clearly not peripheral in terms of the large UK market. Portugal is well placed to serve the Spanish market. Even Greece, which has so far failed to attract much investment from the rest of the Community, may be in a prime location to supply either the Middle East or the Balkan states. What is important is not to see these countries from the viewpoint of the Community. In some cases, the relevant market is much smaller. In other cases, it is not part of the Community at all.

Another point which emerges from the data is the role of integration in encouraging inward investment. America's share of its European investment in Britain fell steadily from one-half in the late 1950s after the formation of the Common Market to one-third in the early 1970s. This decline was not arrested until Britain joined the Community in 1973. Similarly, the Irish share of US FDI doubled in the five years following membership. The accession of Spain and Portugal in the mid-1980s led to a dramatic increase in interest in those countries by investors. A large share of this investment has been in the underdeveloped service sector and in real estate. Membership of the Community for these two countries encourages inward investment to benefit from faster economic growth, greater policy certainty, liberalization of capital flows, deregulation and the removal of trade barriers for both imports and exports.

Until now, we have discussed the pattern of investment without any reference to government policies in individual member states and to the potential role of EC policies, e.g. structural funds. We find both in this chapter and in the Appendix that, with the exception of holding companies and finance affiliates, proximity and market size can explain a good deal of what we observe about firms' behaviour. Nevertheless, in a world where governments actively compete for investment in some areas while restricting it in others, we need to focus more clearly on the effects of government policies. It is to that subject that we now turn.

5

GOVERNMENTS AND FIRMS: POLICIES RELATING TO DIRECT INVESTMENT WITHIN EUROPE

Government policies influence both directly and indirectly where firms locate their activities. In this chapter, we look more carefully at these policies and assess their likely effect on the location choices of firms. Government policies can affect investment patterns in many ways, serving either to attract firms or to prevent them from gaining access to the host market. It is fair to say that all governments welcome the economic activity that follows from inward investment but, equally, all must consider the threat that such investment poses to indigenous firms.

We have argued that much of the direct investment in Europe is market-based, but even if market proximity is crucial there is some flexibility in where firms choose to locate. In the previous chapter, we suggested that such competition for investment is most likely to have an effect within market clusters rather than in the whole of the Single Market. Nevertheless, whether this competition occurs among regions within a country or countries within a region, governments and local authorities have a clear incentive to attract the largest share of mobile investment. Thus, in a narrow sense, there is direct competition among governments to attract firms. In a broader sense, there is competition among rules, i.e. among the full range of government policies which shape the business environment in each country.

At the same time as governments lobby potential investors, they also retain policies and practices which restrict the potential for inward investment as a way of protecting indigenous firms. As the debate on structural impediments shows, it is no longer simply what a government does to restrict market access that matters, but also whether it does anything to remove existing structural impediments. Even if a host country erects no barriers, it may still hamper foreign firms' access to its market by failing to take the necessary steps to break down structural barriers in its economy. If direct investment is an important form of market access, then we need to look carefully at the barriers to investment as well as to trade. In many cases, as we can see from the list below, they are the same.

(a) Barriers or impediments to market access in each specific area:
- Goods: Tariffs, anti-dumping duties, quotas, VERs, customs procedures, technical standards, distance costs, etc.
- Services: Absence of right of establishment or mutual recognition.
- FDI: Capital controls, no national treatment, performance requirements, takeover codes, cross-shareholdings and capital market structure, local content requirements.*

(b) Barriers to market access in all three areas (for foreign or domestic firms):

Monopolistic or oligopolistic market structure, state ownership or subsidies to domestic firms, heavy regulation, public procurement practices.

(c) Policies which promote local production (foreign- or domestically-owned):

Trade barriers, liberal regulatory regime, subsidies, tax incentives, infrastructure support, local content requirements.*

In this chapter, we will discuss some of these policy variables to assess their likely impact on the distribution of investment in Europe. We will begin with a review of the dramatic policy shifts relating to inward and outward investment which have occurred in almost all industrialized countries.

The international context
Developments within the EC must be seen in the context of an international trend towards liberalization of capital controls and market deregulation during the 1980s. The measures undertaken in the EC, such as the full elimination of capital controls through the 1988 Directive on the free movement of capital within the EC, formed part of this. A recent report by the OECD (1992a) describes how during the 1960s and 1970s a

---

*The effect of local content requirements will depend on other inducements to invest, such as market size or trade policies. If a firm is considering investing rather than exporting, then low local content requirements may speed up the investment. In contrast, high requirements may slow down the investment by making the initial outlay prohibitively high.

number of countries, such as Britain, Germany, Italy, the Netherlands and the United States, had relatively liberal policies, while France, Spain, Sweden and others had comprehensive examination procedures on inward investment or capital controls on outward investment.

In the late 1970s Britain and the United States led the way to a further liberalization of capital controls and deregulation of previously regulated sectors such as financial services and air transport, thus creating market pressure for liberalization in other countries so as to be able to compete for footloose inward FDI. The removal of capital controls also enabled firms in liberal countries to compete in foreign markets, which in turn led to policy changes by countries that had hitherto supported national champion strategies based in part in controls on outward FDI. In other words, as some companies were allowed to compete globally by the removal of capital controls, the more restrictive governments were obliged to follow suit. The general liberalization that occurred is reflected in the growth in inward and outward FDI in the 1980s described in Chapter 2. The difficulty comes in trying to isolate the effects of different national policies.

Within the EC the member states most affected by the 1988 Directive were France, which had retained some controls, and Spain and Portugal, which benefited from an exemption from the full liberalization provisions of the Directive until the end of 1992, with a possible extension until 1995 for Portugal. Also affected were Denmark, Italy and Ireland, which had less important capital controls. The 1988 Directive probably contributed to the rapid growth in outward investment from France as French companies were allowed to compete freely on international markets through FDI. French companies were the most active in cross-border acquisition business between 1988 and 1991. The liberalization of capital controls also seems to coincide with the dramatic growth in FDI out of Sweden (see Table 2.2). Sweden had significant controls until 1985 but liberalized them progressively during the second half of the 1980s.

National subsidies and Community control efforts

Patterns of subsidization
Provisions aimed at enhancing the transparency of national aid schemes have enabled fairly good-quality data to be gathered on the level and form of national subsidies within the EC.[1] The total nominal level of aid to manufacturing in the EC was some 34 billion ecus in 1990 or 3.3 percent of value added in manufacturing. Although the Community only began a

Figure 5.1 State aid to the manufacturing sector (as percentage of valucd added)

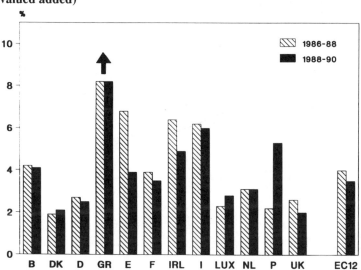

Source: European Commission.

systematic inventory of state aid in 1986, there is some indication of a decline in the importance of aid over time (see Figure 5.1). This trend is consistent with the overall decrease in the level of subsidization in OECD countries. Work carried out by the OECD (1992c) suggests that the level of subsidies has been falling generally, from 3.3 per cent of manufacturing GDP in 1986 for the whole of the OECD to 1.8 per cent in 1989.

Figure 5.1 shows that, within the Community, the level of aid varies dramatically, from 2 per cent of value added in manufacturing in Britain to 6 per cent in Italy (figures for Greece may be higher but are not reliable). Such comparisons require further qualification, as the types of aid vary almost as much as the levels across countries. Most aid is provided in the form of direct financial transfers (47 per cent) and investment tax incentives (32 per cent), with equity participation through public enterprises (7 per cent), soft loans (7 per cent) and guarantees (6 per cent) much less important.

Table 5.1 reveals that much of this aid goes for horizontal (general) schemes, such as aid for innovation or export (some 42 per cent of total aid to manufacturing in the EC) or to specific regions (38 per cent), but less to particular sectors (20 per cent). A high proportion of aid is provided in the core areas of the Community, with Italy, Germany,

Table 5.1 State aid to manufacturing by sector and function, 1988–90

Sector/function	B	DK	D	GR	E	F	IRL	I	L	NL	P	UK	EUR12
Horizontal objectives	76	59	29	81	28	66	50	30	39	77	17	45	42
Innovation; R+D	13	35	12	1	9	17	4	4	8	35	1	8	10
Environment	0	4	2	0	1	0	0	0	1	2	0	2	1
Small & medium-sized enterprises	25	1	7	10	5	11	8	10	21	31	0	12	10
Trade/export	14	8	2	22	1	36	38	6	2	1	0	15	11
Economization of energy	6	10	3	0	1	1	0	1	0	2	0	0	1
General investment	12	0	0	10	5	1	0	2	8	4	1	9	3
General objectives	6	0	2	37	6	0	0	7	0	0	14	0	5
Particular sectors	4	38	11	5	67	25	9	15	0	11	78	20	20
Shipbuilding	1	32	3	3	10	4	0	4	0	7	27	7	5
Other sectors	3	6	8	2	57	21	9	11	0	4	51	13	15
Regional objectives	21	3	61	15	5*	9	42	55	61	12	5	34	38
Regions under 92(3)c	21	3	9	—	—	5	—	4	61	12	—	25	8
Regions under 92(3)a	—	—		15	5	4	42	51	—	—	5	9	30
Berlin/92(2)a			52										
Total	100	100	100	100	100	100	100	100	100	100	100	100	100

Source: Commission of the European Communities (1992b).
*Subdivision not available.
92(3)a = support for regions below specific levels of GDP.
92(3)c = regional support for areas affected by industrial structural problems.

France and Britain accounting for 75 per cent of all aid. Indeed some of the most significant reductions in recent years (measured in terms of total aid as a percentage of GDP) have been in peripheral regions of the EC such as Spain and Ireland.

If one discounts sectoral support, which tends to go to maintain existing production and which does not therefore directly attract new investment, some 80 per cent of the aid to manufacturing could have an impact on FDI either into a particular economy (horizontal schemes) or to a particular region.[2] Because sectoral support represents such a high proportion of aid by Spain and Portugal (67 and 78 per cent respectively), the weight of general incentives which might attract FDI remains very much in the central core of the EC.

Regional aid schemes
In 1988, the Commission defined two kinds of regions within which regional aid is permitted: those where GDP per capita is below 75 per cent of the EC average (namely the whole of Ireland, Portugal and Greece, the French overseas departments, the Mezziogiorno in Italy, much of southern, western and central Spain, and Northern Ireland); and those affected by the decline of specific industries, such as textiles, steel and shipbuilding. Permissible aid as a percentage of investment ranges from 75 per cent in the Highlands and Islands of Scotland to 7 per cent in parts of northern Italy, but most rates are in the 15–30 per cent range.

At a Community level, there is a desire to channel investment to peripheral regions to promote EC-wide cohesion. But this is hindered by the growth of horizontal schemes such as those promoting innovation or exports. EC policy was initially aimed at containing competition between locations in the provision of regional aid, but to be effective the Commission has been obliged to seek tighter control of horizontal schemes. Such schemes can easily provide core locations in the Community with more favourable benefits than the peripheral regions. Gilchrist and Deacon (1990) of the European Commission have argued for a shift in policy in recognition of this problem.

In spite of the obvious disadvantages faced by the peripheral areas, it is difficult to generalize about the effectiveness of regional incentives from overall levels of aid, since well-targeted aid could still help to ensure that footloose investment is attracted at relatively little expense. From our discussion in earlier chapters, it should not come as a surprise that regional policy has been ineffective at an overall Community level, since market clusters may be more important than policy variables in determining the location of production for export. To the extent that incentives are effective, they are most likely to influence firms that have already decided to invest in a particular cluster or national market.

The effectiveness of regional aid is hampered because it must compete both against other forms of subsidies and against similar aid offered by other potential locations. Nevertheless, there is some indication that regional aid can influence investment decisions within certain large national markets, and such incentives are generally viewed as a necessary form of social policy. For the same policy to be effective in the Community as a whole, the Commission must strive both to reduce other forms of subsidies and to ensure that competition for footloose investment does not work to the detriment of peripheral areas.

Treaty provisions and their implementation
To what extent has the Commission been successful in controlling and reducing general subsidies within the Community? The European Community has extensive powers to control national subsidies under the provisions of the Treaties of Rome (Articles 92 and 93 (EEC)) and Paris (Articles 4 and 54 (ECSC)) to ban *all* national subsidies. The basic approach set out in the Treaties was that there should be a general prohibition on subsidies but with provisions for exemptions (Art. 93 (EEC) and 95 (ECSC)). In 1971 the Commission sought to improve the transparency of national subsidies and to clamp down on those in the core areas of the EC, i.e. on competitive subsidies across common borders such as between France and Germany.[3] After further minor modifications during the 1970s the Commission fully revised the guidelines in 1988, stipulating which areas qualified for regional aid.

As national governments shifted funding to horizontal schemes, the Commission introduced guidelines such as those for research and development aid (1988), which distinguish between basic research, where permissible aid intensity can be 50 per cent or higher (in the case of small and medium-sized companies), and applied research and development, where aid intensity is lower the closer the project is to the market.[4] There are also guidelines for environmental aid programmes, which permit a 15 per cent aid intensity.

In addition to the general aid schemes there has been a long tradition of sectoral aid policies. These apply treaty provisions to the sector concerned and have generally been introduced in response to a particular crisis, such as in textiles, steel, man-made fibres and shipbuilding, in which surplus capacity has resulted in intervention by various member states to aid the same sector. While such subsidies usually tend to maintain production, adjustment assistance, aimed at attracting new jobs to an area affected by plant closures, is included under sectoral aid schemes and thus can be used to lure inward investors.

The Commission's policy towards national subsidies was criticized initially as too ad hoc, and in response the Commission sought to increase transparency by initiating a series of reviews of existing national aid schemes. The transparency effort resulted in the regular surveys of aid starting in 1989;[5] systematic reviews are now conducted, resulting in a number of schemes being discontinued.[6]

The latest Commission initiative has been to enhance transparency and control of aid to public enterprises via the provision of public equity capital, accounting for some 7 per cent of national subsidies.[7] Despite opposition from a number of member states, especially Britain and France, the Commission's policy found support in the European Court of Justice (ECJ), and the Commission has subsequently introduced 1991 guidelines on the application of the treaty to public companies based on the 'market economy investor principle'. In other words, if the state invests when the private market operators would not there is a degree of subsidization.[8] The principle covers the criteria under which capital injections, guarantees or loans provided by the state to public enterprises are assessed by the Commission. Capital injections for public enterprise do not attract inward FDI but can promote outward FDI and have been an issue in certain acquisitions by French companies of English water companies, see below. According to the Commission's figures, however, the general level of subsidy in capital injections into public enterprises is low.

The existence of provisions which enable the Commission to control national subsidies does not guarantee effective control. For many years, the political environment did not allow interventionist Commission policies in spite of existing treaty powers because no member state was willing to deny itself the right to provide subsidies. Even Britain, one of the most liberal countries, and the one with the lowest level of subsidies, waited until well into the 1980s (and the disposal of companies like Rover) before supporting a tough EC control of national subsidies.

Community policy has begun to have more effect on national subsidy programmes, but it is difficult to ascribe the general reduction in national subsidies, if indeed there has been one, to the tougher Community controls. National governments have probably been reducing aid levels for budgetary or other policy reasons. The Commission may not be able (or wish) to make significant reductions in the level of subsidy but its policies do encourage national governments to adhere to a common set of rules.[9] The Commission has also succeeded in confirming the comprehensive nature of EC controls. Thus guidelines on how the treaties should be implemented now cover more and more activities, including such areas as R&D support and public enterprise capitalization in which national governments have had a free hand until very recently.

The overall level of subsidy in individual countries is poorly correlated with the amount of inward investment that they receive. Britain has the lowest level of aid but still attracts a significant level of inward intra-EC investment. Greece and Ireland provide relatively high levels of aid but attract only a small proportion of intra-EC FDI. The apparent absence of inward FDI into Germany is not explained by an absence of subsidies, as Germany provides a fairly high level of subsidies. Italy seems to provide high levels of predominantly regional as opposed to horizontal support for very little return. But it may be necessary to consider a situation in which the causality of subsidy and investment is reversed. For example, subsidies may be provided because the structural economic characteristics of a particular location are poor. Thus Germany may provide subsidies because it is unsuccessful in attracting investment and Britain may well have been able to cut subsidies because it was able to attract investment for other reasons. This does not argue against the case that subsidies have only a limited impact. For example, it would be consistent to argue that subsidies cannot by themselves compensate for poor structural features. But it may help to explain why countries that have little FDI also have relatively high levels of subsidy.

Unfortunately, for this exercise, the overall level of subsidies may bear little relation to specific incentives to inward investors. We cannot distinguish between the two in the available data. Nevertheless, there does appear to be strong competition among member states to attract investment, most notably in the case of Japanese firms. To what extent has the Commission succeeded in reducing this bidding war? Unfortunately, not enough has been done. The Commission has sought to control the larger subsidies in the core member states such as support for the car industry in France. As in the past this has created resentment on the part of governments providing subsidies, and has strengthened the subsidiarity debate in defence of national policies and in opposition to Commission controls. For the sake of competition within the EC it is important that subsidiarity is not so abused. Nevertheless there are difficult questions concerning the activist role of the Directorate on competition, cartels and state aids (DGIV). Can it, for example, intervene in smaller cases in which local or regional governments provide support for local investment? If it does it is likely to be accused of being heavy-handed and overbearing. But it may be precisely such marginal supports that have the most effect on investment decisions.

As with more general subsidies, competition between subsidy programmes will probably decline when individual countries decide unilaterally that the benefits from these subsidies in terms of, say, jobs created are quite small. Ireland, one of the leading promoters of inward investment as a form of industrial policy, is finally beginning to question the cost-effectiveness of its incentives and is turning more towards the fostering of indigenous industry. A more activist DGIV has nevertheless probably helped to contain competitive subsidization. National or regional authorities can more easily resist pressure for subsidies by referring to EC rules which ensure that a competing location is not threatening to outbid.

The effects of different tax regimes on FDI

Tax breaks such as tax holidays or tax-based investment incentives may influence investment and are an important means by which countries such as Germany, Ireland and Italy provide incentives. The totals for subsidies in the previous section included these tax incentives. But taxation can affect investment in other ways, such as through its differential impact on profits retained for direct investment in other member states relative to investment in the home country.

In spite of an overall decline in the average EC corporation tax from 46 per cent in 1985 to 40 per cent in 1991, corporation tax rates differ widely within the Community. National rates (including national and local corporation tax) vary from 50 per cent in Germany to 34 per cent in Britain. Italy and Greece also have fairly high rates of corporation tax (see Table 5.2). At first sight high corporation tax might be expected to discourage FDI and thus might help to explain the low level of inward FDI into the high-tax countries. But the picture is more complex. It is important to compare high rates of corporation tax with the level of subsidy provided through tax deductions. Germany, Italy and Ireland have high taxes but also provide many tax incentives. In contrast Britain has a low level of corporation tax but provides virtually no tax based investment incentives; this reflects a conscious policy decision, taken in the mid-1980s, to reduce both tax rates and incentives for investment. High corporate taxes and tax incentives may offset each other.

Table 5.2 Overall (national and local) corporate tax rates in the EC (%)[1]

	1980	1985	1991[2]
Belgium	48	45	39
Denmark	37	50	38
Germany	61.7/44.3	61.7/44.3	57.5/45.6
Greece	—	49	46(40)[3]
Spain	33	33	35.3
France	50	50	34/42
Ireland	45	50(10)[4]	43(10)[4]
Italy	36.3	47.8/36	47.8/36
Luxembourg	45.5	45.5	39.4
Netherlands	46	42	35
Portugal	51.2/44	51.2/44	39.6
UK	52	40	34
EC average	46.0	46.9	40.1
(standard	(7.8)	(7.0)	(6.7)
deviation)			
Austria	61.5/38.3	61.5/38.3	39
Canada	42.4	51.6	41.7(35.7)[4]
Japan	52.0/42.0	55.4/45.4	50
Sweden	40	52	30
Switzerland	11.7 to 36.6[5]	12.3 to 35.0[5]	13.2 to 38.4[5]
USA	49.2	49.5	38.3

Source: Ruding Committee.

[1]Where two rates are given, the former reflects the tax rate on retentions, the latter the tax rate on distributions. The averages and standard deviations for the Community are calculated on the basis of retained profits, and exclude Greece.

[2]Rates at 1.1.1991.

[3]A lower tax rate (40% in 1991) applies where companies are quoted on the Athens Stock Exchange.

[4]Figure in brackets is the tax rate on manufacturing industry.

[5]Progressive rate schedule.

Member states also differ in their tax treatment of domestic and foreign investment, often to the detriment of cross-border FDI. The key elements of these differences are the level of withholding tax on dividends paid and the tax treatment of earnings from subsidiaries abroad. The considerable amount of work done on this issue has been summarized in a recent Commission-sponsored report on the impact of tax treatment on investment within the EC – the so-called Ruding Committee Report. Drawing together much of the existing material and also adding its own survey and research data, the Committee assessed the degree to which the EC diverged from the ideal of neutrality in tax treatment of

Table 5.3 Average cost of capital for transnational investment[1]

		Average cost of capital[2]		Standard deviation	
	Domestic (source = residence)	Residence (investment from named country into others)	Source (investment into named country from others)	Residence	Source
Belgium	5.4	6.5	6.6	0.7	0.5
Denmark	5.8	6.1	6.9	0.4	0.9
Germany	5.6	7.3	6.1	1.1	0.4
Greece	5.1	7.9	7.0	1.3	2.1
Spain	6.1	6.6	8.0	0.3	2.1
France	5.4	6.2	7.6	0.5	1.1
Ireland	5.1	8.6	6.7	2.9	1.5
Italy	6.0	8.0	7.1	1.1	0.8
Luxembourg	6.2	6.6	7.0	0.5	0.9
Netherlands	5.7	6.5	7.0	0.8	1.5
Portugal	5.7	8.0	7.9	1.6	2.1
UK	5.9	6.4	6.8	0.4	0.8
EC average	5.7	7.1	7.1	1.0	1.2
Austria	5.3	6.7	6.7	0.5	1.1
Canada	6.1	7.1	8.2	0.7	1.6
Japan	6.5	7.6	8.2	0.4	1.6
Sweden	5.0	6.5	6.4	0.5	1.5
Switzerland	5.5	6.4	6.7	0.6	1.0
USA	5.9	6.7	7.5	0.4	1.7

[1]Assuming the subsidiary is financed by one-third retentions by the subsidiary, one-third new equity from the parent and one-third debt from the parent; investment in a weighted average set of assets: inflation of 3.1% everywhere; personal taxes are zero; parent raises finance in a weighted average of debt, new shares and retained earnings.
[2]Averages for EC countries are based on investment to and from other EC countries. Averages for non-EC countries are based on investments into and from the EC countries.

investment across borders. Table 5.3 summarizes the findings. It shows that all member states of the EC, as well as other OECD countries, discriminate against outward FDI by indigenous firms in their tax regimes (second column compared with first column) as well as against inward FDI compared with domestic investment (third column compared with first column). For example, the pre-tax return on domestic investment needed to achieve a five per cent post-tax return on capital invested in Belgium is 5.4 per cent, but a Belgian company investing abroad must earn 6.5 per cent in order to make the same post-tax return. A company investing in Belgium has to earn 6.6 per cent in order to make a 5 per cent return. Note that all countries discriminate against outward and inward FDI, but in some the standard deviation (columns 4 and 5) is higher than in others. Germany, Greece, Ireland, Italy and Portugal discriminate more than the EC average on outward investment. In the case of the peripheral countries this is in part an effort to retain limited domestic capital: such countries have also used capital controls in the past for the same purpose. But this cannot be said to be the case with Germany. The standard deviation in the case of Britain, Benelux and Spain is below the EC average.

Differences in the tax treatment of investment across the Community result in a highly complex matrix of bilateral tax relationships which may influence investment. For example, a Belgian company investing in Denmark must earn 6.7 per cent before tax in order to have a post-tax return of 5 per cent. Company surveys carried out by Ruding and others found that tax treatment is becoming a more important factor in investment decisions as other barriers come down. An Irish company investing in Spain must earn 14.2 per cent pre-tax, while a Portuguese company investing in Spain needs only 7 per cent pre-tax in order to have post-tax earnings of 5 per cent. The return on investment also depends on how the investment is financed. Most of the differences between the treatment of local and cross-border investment are accounted for by differences in the tax treatment of debt- as opposed to equity-financed FDI. Once again the smaller member states find the cost of borrowed capital higher than those with large, liberalized capital markets like Britain, France, Belgium and the Netherlands. The oddity is Germany, where the cost of borrowed capital on outward FDI is relatively high. This is potentially a significant deterrent in an economy in which debt is an important source of industrial finance.

The Ruding Committee Report (1992, p. 97) concluded that there was evidence that tax treatment had a non-negligible impact on investment but it was not clear just how to quantify that impact. Additional survey results based on the responses of some 650 companies with cross-border investment in the EC led the Ruding Committee to argue that 'cross border tax differentials are rarely the main driving force behind non-financial investment although [they] may be more important for financial investment.'

Japanese and German banking investment in Luxembourg and holding companies in the Netherlands all relate partly to the favourable tax treatment accorded to such operations in those countries, just as Delaware is the first choice of American firms when they wish to incorporate.

Over one-half of the stock of Italian outward investment is in Luxembourg, the Netherlands and Switzerland. Although substantial amounts of capital are reported to flow to and from these countries as a result of these financial operations, it is unlikely that such flows bear any resemblance to what is typically meant by foreign direct investment. Affiliates in those countries are simply a convenient place to channel profits and have little effect on the distribution of investment within Europe.

As the Ruding Committee testified, the extent to which differing tax treatment influences the allocation of real economic activities within the Community is difficult to assess. Given the range of influences on outward and inward investment mentioned in earlier chapters, it would be foolish to attribute too large a role to differing tax rates. There are few Portuguese firms capable of investing in Denmark, no matter how favourable the tax treatment. Nevertheless, it is almost certain that differing methods and levels of taxation do discourage firms from venturing abroad, particularly when they are small. A survey conducted by the Ruding Committee found that business viewed the tax treatment of cross-border investment as an important factor in investment decisions. For large multinational companies with well-staffed finance departments tax differences are probably much more manageable than for smaller firms. As larger firms tend to carry out more investment than smaller firms the impact on overall investment flows may be less pronounced even if there is a bias against cross-border investment.

Convergence

One of the central questions addressed by the Ruding Committee was whether EC policy initiatives were needed in order to reduce the discrimination in tax treatment or whether competition between tax regimes would bring about a convergence through market forces. As Table 5.2 indicated, there has been some convergence and some reduction of the levels of corporate taxation in the EC, resulting at least partly from competition among locations. For example, when Germany sought to introduce a withholding tax (of 25 per cent) on investment income there was significant capital flight, mainly to the Luxembourg subsidiaries of German banks, where there was no withholding tax. When other member states refused to harmonize withholding taxes, arguing that funds would go to Switzerland, Bonn was forced to back down. On balance, however, the Ruding Committee concluded that there was no evidence of competition between regimes resulting in a general erosion of tax levels. The reductions observed in Table 5.2 were, it argued, more to do with a decline in inflation over the second half of the 1980s. There is, in any case, less evidence of convergence between the different national regimes when it comes to the treatment of earnings from foreign subsidiaries.

Interaction with integration
International, not just EC, market pressure has probably led to some convergence of base rates for corporation tax as a result of competition between member states for investment. Generally speaking, however, the Single Market process has not yet had much impact on the differences in tax treatment discussed above. A desire for fiscal sovereignty on the part of most national governments has held up EC directives on direct taxation. The Commission has, however, produced two draft directives on the treatment of profits from foreign subsidiaries and withholding taxes. The former seeks to reduce the discrimination against FDI within the EC by enabling companies with subsidiaries in other member states to offset losses from these subsidiaries against profits of the parent company. At present it is only possible to offset losses from a subsidiary within the home state but not from a foreign subsidiary; thus there is discrimination against outward investment.

The Ruding Committee was asked to consider whether investment within the EC was affected by tax treatment and, if so, to make recommendations about what should be done. It found that distortion takes place, although it has not been possible to quantify it. The Committee recommended that the existing directives should be strengthened and implemented and that there should ultimately be a harmonization of corporation tax. In the meantime the unfavourable tax treatment of cross-border FDI will continue to be one factor deterring intra-EC direct investment and hence limiting the potential benefits to home and host countries and to the EC as a whole from further integration.

Labour costs and social policy
A major rationale for Britain's opposition to the social dimension of the integration process in the EC is that it would make Britain and the rest of the EC less competitive, and result in a loss of FDI. Indeed when Prime Minister Major concluded the Maastricht negotiations which provided for Britain to opt out of the social chapter of the European Union, he argued that Britain would become a mecca for Japanese FDI. But the key determinants of labour costs, namely wages and social security payments, are not affected by the Community's social policy.

There is no EC-level collective bargaining nor any real prospect of it developing in the near future. Employers are strongly opposed to any such moves and are supported in their opposition by the centre or centre-right governments in the EC. Within the unions there has been division between more corporatist approaches, as in Germany and the Netherlands, and the more confrontational style which has prevailed in other countries. In recent years the unions have shifted ground, in part as a result of the internal market programme or rather a realization that national strategies are no longer viable. This has led to more interest on the part of the unions and more support for the European Trades Union Congress (ETUC) in its initiatives to begin some form of dialogue with employers' organizations at the EC level. As a result of this change in attitude and the support of the Commission under Delors, an agreement was reached at Maastricht which could encourage more dialogue. But this dialogue will be focused on social regulation rather than wages.

The impact of the EC on social regulation, such as maximum working hours and common provisions on unsocial working hours and maternity leave, etc., will be quite limited in terms of labour costs. Table 3.1 showed that the main element of non-wage costs is social security payments. These will not be affected by the social action programme or the social chapter agreed by the Eleven at Maastricht. Even the Eleven agree that changes to social security provisions should require unanimity. It is therefore unlikely that EC directives will accelerate labour cost convergence. Market pressures resulting from the integration of markets for goods and services, together with reductions in labour cost fluctuations, seem more likely to bring about a convergence throughout the 1990s than EC policies.

The social action programme of the EC includes proposals on an Information and Consultation Directive, which would establish European Works Councils, promoting the development of Europe-wide bargaining within firms. But there are formidable barriers to any industry- or economy-wide collective bargaining both within the structures of employee representation and trade unions across the EC and in the determined opposition of employers. In other words, the two main components of differences in labour costs across the EC are unlikely to be affected by EC integration in the medium or even long term.

Barriers to takeover

Given that mergers and acquisitions probably account for a significant share of intra-EC FDI, policy measures or other factors that affect mergers and acquisitions could strongly affect FDI. Britain ranks highly as a target country in terms of M&As, much as it does for FDI, while, allowing for a possible bias in the reporting, Germany is under-represented in the total figures for local acquisitions by foreign firms. Such a finding is consistent with the conventional view of the relative openness of the two capital markets.

In broad terms Britain has an environment most conducive to takeovers, with a more or less fully open market for corporate control. The rest of the EC is characterized by either structural or technical barriers to takeovers. In the southern member states such as Italy, Spain and to some extent France, the barriers to takeover relate to the *structure* of ownership and control, such as cross-shareholdings or state shareholdings, or to the fact that many companies, including the major ones, are still effectively under family control. In the northern member states such as Germany and the Netherlands, and also in Switzerland, the impediments to takeover largely take the form of *technical* barriers which make it difficult to gain control of companies,[10] such as company law and stock market rules which allow companies to issue large numbers of non-voting shares and thus raise capital without diluting control of the company.

Capital markets

As noted in Chapter 2, the size (and openness) of capital markets is correlated with the volume of foreign direct investment flows. The British capital market, measured as total capitalization as a percentage of GDP, is around 100 per cent, compared with 40–50 per cent for the Netherlands and only 20 per cent for Germany and France or around 15 per cent for Italy and Spain. A large open capital market means an open market for takeovers and an ability to finance foreign acquisitions. The size of Britain's capital market, and to some extent that of the Netherlands, therefore helps to explain the high levels of inward and outward investment in these countries relative to Germany or Italy. German outward investment was the highest in Europe in 1991 though it remains low relative to the size of its market. France has been moving towards a larger, more open capital market which has increased the number of acquisitions and in particular the use of hostile takeovers. In Germany and Italy there are still very few hostile takeovers.

Method of financing investment

The existence of a large capital market is related to the fact that share capital is more important as a source of finance in Britain than in other countries, where debt or bank finance is more prevalent. This is also reflected in the number of publicly listed companies in each of the countries concerned. There are some 2,500 companies listed on the London stock exchange, compared with about 450 in France (on a rising trend) and 400 in the various German exchanges and Spain, and only about 200 in Italy. What is more, there are important cross-shareholdings among many Italian companies, which means that restructuring requires the support of a group of companies. In France the state retains 15 per cent of shares despite the privatization of many companies during the 1980s.

The ownership structure

The structure of ownership is also important. In the UK there are large institutional shareholdings, and funds managed by pension funds etc. tend to have a more arm's-length relationship with companies. By contrast, in Italy family ownership and cross-shareholdings remain important. As a result Coopers & Lybrand (1989) have estimated that of the 200 companies listed on the Milan stock exchange perhaps only 7 are truly public companies that could be bought. Public enterprise also accounts for a sizeable share of Italian industry. Faced with rigidities and the need to reduce public debt in order to meet the convergence criteria for European Monetary Union, the Italian state is contemplating major reform of its public enterprises.

The structure of ownership in Germany also militates against an open form of restructuring. In the case of large as well as small firms there is often a close identification of interests among the stakeholders in the company, i.e. the investors who are often large financial institutions, employees and the local communities within which firms have invested. The holistic German approach differs significantly from the arm's-length relationship between the company and the stakeholders in Britain.

Similar structural barriers exist in France, where the top 40 companies – which account for over 60 per cent of the total market capitalization – are not for sale, either because of family control or cross-shareholdings, or because of the operation of the *noyau dur* (shares of previously publicly-owned companies which were distributed among a number of French companies in order to ensure an effective defence against unwanted foreign bids). The opening up of the French capital market has fostered a debate about the need to strengthen defences against 'Anglo-Saxon' hostile takeovers.

Technical barriers to control
Compared with Italy, the structure of ownership in Germany and the Netherlands is still fairly open. Fewer companies are protected as a result of cross-shareholdings, although, interestingly, family/trust control has remained fairly important in Germany despite the size of some of the companies involved and the level of development of the economy. There is, nevertheless, a general tendency for the existing ownership and management of companies to defend their interests by placing hurdles in the path of any acquirer. For instance, a shareholder, even with a 50 per cent ownership of a company, may be restricted to 10 per cent of the voting rights. Loss of control is also prevented or hindered by the issue of non-voting shares or by subsidiaries buying the shares of a parent company. All such practices are prohibited by the British regulatory authorities (i.e. the Takeover Panel on takeovers and the Stock Exchange with regard to listing requirements). The hostile acquisition and deconglomeration through sale of assets, such as occurs as part of everyday life in the City of London, is a further example of the Anglo-Saxon approach. In Germany and the Netherlands regulation and practice do not put the interests of the shareholders above those of any other stakeholder in the company, and in the Netherlands 'white knight' pacts, in which a group of companies agree to help each other by acquiring shares, defend firms against hostile bids.

These various barriers to takeover result from established national practices and ownership structures. They reflect an underlying desire to maintain continuity in corporate governance and not to see regular changes of ownership, particularly in Germany. In France at the beginning of the 1980s the combined effect of national champion policies and nationally-oriented corporate strategies meant that the leading French companies had a much lower level of internationalization than many of their foreign rivals. There has been a progressive liberalization and some Anglo-Saxon methods are beginning to find their way into the French system, with takeovers becoming more common. French companies, including publicly-owned ones, have also expanded their cross-border merger and acquisition activity throughout the EC and globally in order to catch up in terms of their international presence.

The completion of a single market for goods and services will not mean an end to national industrial identity. In many member states there remains a residual desire to defend national industrial sovereignty which may well explain why most countries are less than enthusiastic about the idea of creating a level playing-field for takeovers. Mergers and acquisitions in much of continental Europe are often mutually agreed between firms. The recent *accord cadre* (framework agreement) between Fiat and Ahlstrom/GEC, in which the two groups proposed swapping affiliates in order to concentrate on (different) core activities, is an example of a less open approach.

Assessment

This section has discussed not only the relative openness of the national markets for corporate control, which is itself a factor of the size of capital markets, but also the structural and technical barriers to takeover that exist in various countries. Britain has both the largest capital market and the most open market for corporate control. As a result the value of inward acquisitions exceeds that of outward in Britain by a factor of four. The only country with a higher ratio of inward to outward acquisitions is Spain, which makes virtually no acquisitions abroad. Britain accounted for 32 per cent by value of all inward acquisitions within the EC in 1991. At the other extreme is Italy, where the ratio of outward to inward acquisitions in value terms is 4:1, reflecting the low level of acquisitions of Italian firms. French acquisitions abroad were twice the value of foreign acquisitions in France in 1991, and the ratio for Germany was 1.3:1. Similar patterns can be found for earlier years.[11] In other words there would seem to be a correlation between the size and openness of capital markets and FDI. Britain's large open capital market means that takeovers are used for industrial restructuring, while the existence of structural or technical barriers to takeover in Germany and Italy may help to explain why the level of inward FDI is so low in these countries. In continental Europe as a whole mergers and acquisitions occur but they are controlled by the companies concerned, presumably on the basis of industrial rationales, rather than being determined by financial criteria as is much more often the case in Britain.

The impact of EC policy

The European Commission has made a number of proposals aimed at removing barriers to takeover within the internal market. Indeed much of the impetus for legislative proposals concerning company law and takeovers initially came from the British government, which was at pains to ensure a level playing-field for acquisitions across the EC. Company law directives, such as the Fifth Company Law Directive, would remove

Table 5.4 Monopolies and concessions

Country	1	2	3	4	5
Australia	P		P	P/Pr	P/PR
Austria	P		Co	Co	Co
Belgium	P		P/Pr	P	Pr
Canada	P/Pr*				P/Pr
Denmark	P/Co	Co	Co		Co
Finland	P/Pr	P	P		Pr
France	P	Co	P		P
Germany	P/M	P/Co	P/Co		
Greece	P		P	P	P
Iceland	P				P
Ireland	P		P	M	P
Italy	P	Co	P		P
Japan	P				
Luxembourg	P	P			P
Netherlands	P	Pr	P/Pr		P
New Zealand	P		P		P
Norway	P	P/Co*	P/Co	Co	P/Co
Portugal	P/Co		P	P	P
Spain	P/Pr	Co	P/M/Co		P
Sweden	P	P			
Switzerland	P	M	P/M	M	
Turkey	P	P	P		P
United Kingdom	P/M		P		P/M*
United States	P/Pr				P/M*

P = Public Pr = Private M = Mixed private / public Co = Concession
* Monopolies or concessions at the subnational level
1 Telecommunications (including postal and telephone service and satellite system telecommunications)
2 Broadcasting (including publishing, radio and television)
3 Land transport (including railways)
4 Air transport
5 Public utilities (including energy, water, gas and electricity distributions)
NB This table shows the existence of public, private or mixed public/private monopolies for some or all of the activities covered by the sectors listed. Thus more than one mark may appear where different activities in one sector are subject to different types of monopoly.

some of the more blatant legal barriers to takeover by, for example, removing the right to limit shareholders' voting rights or the ability of a subsidiary to purchase shares of a parent company (as in the Second Company Law Directive). There are also proposals for a Thirteenth Company Law Directive, which would introduce a common takeover regime based on the British code on takeovers. But these are being blocked – not least by the British government, which wants neither the provisions on employee representation attached to the directives nor a change in the voluntary nature of the City Takeover Panel, which would be subject to judicial review by the ECJ. Even if these directives were to be adopted, their impact on the openness of the markets for corporate control would be limited since it depends much more on deep-seated systemic factors. Here, therefore, as in other areas of policy, EC integration is unlikely to bring about any rapid convergence.

Liberalization and structural barriers

Within the EC there are very few remaining statutory barriers to investment. France and Italy retain certain notification requirements following the investment, and Britain retains statutory powers, in the shape of the 1975 Industry Act, to block any investment in British manufacturing industry, although it has never used them. The residual statutory barriers are in a number of sector-specific policies which affect more or less the same sectors in each EC member state, such as transport (maritime and air), fishing and broadcasting. In almost every case EC legislation is eroding the barriers: fishing is a good example. There are more impediments to inward FDI from outside the EC.

Much more important than the residual statutory barriers are structural impediments resulting either from the continued existence of public monopolies or from the legacies of past national champion policies or public and private monopolies. The existence of monopolies in a number of sectors means that there is in reality little prospect of investing. Table 5.4 shows that these are similar in all EC member states and include, among others, broadcasting, telecommunications, land transport and the utilities.

Broadcasting

Few legal restrictions remain on intra-EC investments in broadcasting, but restrictions still apply for non-EC investors.[12] The one major policy instrument that can be used against intra-EC investment in the broadcasting sector is the public policy exemption in the merger control regulation. Article 21 of this regulation allows national governments to block acquisitions or mergers on the grounds of public interest. In other words national governments, which generally have the ultimate responsibility for regulating public broadcasting, can use their discretionary powers to prevent ownership or control passing to a citizen of another EC member state.

Governments and firms: policy issues

Telecommunications

In the past there was no need to have national controls on foreign investment in telecommunications because it was in almost all cases a public monopoly. In the few cases when it was not, a private company was licensed to provide telecommunications services under the control of national authorities. The basic structure of the sector is still dominated by monopolies, although these are now private or mixed in some countries: Britain has privatized, and Germany is planning to sell part of Deutsche Telekom.

EC directives in the telecommunications sector have now liberalized terminal equipment provision and value-added services. There is as yet no directive liberalizing basic voice networks, although this does not prevent some countries, such as the UK, from opening these to competition. In the past it has always been possible to invest in equipment manufacture or service provision but there was little point given that access to the market was barred by the existence of a public monopoly. The liberalization of these parts of the sector has therefore removed a structural impediment to investment. In the case of basic voice networks this impediment still remains. If this part of telecom is liberalized it could result in significantly more FDI than in equipment and services because of the scale of investment concerned.[13]

The utilities

The scale of investment is also massive in the provision of utilities: gas, water and electricity.[14] Again there have been no statutory barriers to entry *per se* in these sectors but the existence of national public or private monopolies has presented an insuperable impediment. There is no point in building a power station unless it can be connected to the grid. These sectors remain essentially closed to foreign investment although some liberalization has occurred. In Britain, for example, the utilities have been privatized and are theoretically for sale. Only France has shown any major interest, in the private water companies and more recently the privatized water suppliers. It was these acquisitions which led the then secretary of state for industry, Peter Lilley, to introduce the so-called 'Lilley doctrine': foreign publicly-owned companies shall not be allowed to acquire private British companies. Such acquisitions were viewed as nationalization via the (European) back door. The Lilley doctrine was opposed by the European Commission, which argued that it was against the provisions of the treaty on free movement of capital and not within the narrowly defined public interest criteria of the merger control regulation, and Mr Lilley had to withdraw his policy.

Land transport
The picture is much the same for railways. Bus services have already been substantially liberalized in some countries in which there were national public operators, although local and regional operators still retain monopolies in many communities. Only Britain has moved towards allowing foreign-owned operators to compete with British Rail. More generally there is a prospect of international operators serving cross-border or long-distance routes on the networks provided by national monopolies. The first attempt at such competition is the SNCF proposal to provide a service through to London via the Channel tunnel.

Air transport
National flag carriers have dominated air transport for many years. Under pressure of increased competition cross-border acquisitions have grown. Liberalization and privatization in Britain have, as in telecommunications, led the way towards more open policies in the EC. British Airways was at one stage bidding for Sabena World Airways. Even Air France is now considering joint ventures and Lufthansa is, along with the German Railways, on Bonn's list of public enterprises for privatization.

Defence industries
As with broadcasting, there are provisions in the merger control directive enabling national authorities to block acquisitions of shares in defence industries on grounds of national public interest. When this provision was being drawn up in 1989 there was considerable debate about how broad the national public interest exemption should be. In the end the provision was narrowly defined and specific reference made to broadcasting, national security (i.e. the defence industry) and prudential security (in banking). The prudential control provisions will soon be largely overtaken by EC directives setting out standards for prudential control.

Appraisal
The continued existence of structural barriers in the shape of public or private monopolies is one of the more important remaining barriers to investment within the EC – more important, for example, than remaining statutory barriers. Of all the member states Britain has moved furthest and fastest to privatize and, in some cases, to liberalize those sectors, moves which could well have had an impact on both inward and outward investment. For example, there is anecdotal evidence that companies engaged in information-intensive activities are investing in Britain

because of the liberal environment, and lower prices, for international communications. Privatization has also removed constraints on companies such as British Telecom or British Airways from becoming active players in foreign markets: hence BT's initiative with mobile communications across the EC and the acquisition by British Airways of US Air. Thus member states which have liberalized their natural monopolies may well have stimulated both inward and outward FDI. This may partly explain Britain's leading position in FDI, as well as the lack of inward FDI into Germany, which has retained a relatively highly regulated control over the utilities and, until recently, over sectors such as telecommunications.

The dynamic effects
The creation of the Single Market involves both market-led and policy-led changes to the environment within which investment takes place. While the two together provided the momentum for the liberalization process in 1988/9 they do not necessarily always coincide. Thus market-led changes, in the shape of corporate decisions to establish a presence across the whole EC, have in most cases preceded the adoption and implementation of policy decisions. This means that while the decision to invest may be based on expectations of market opening, the practical form of investment must take account of the current reality, and the current reality in sectors only recently affected by the EC is one of national market characteristics and market structures established when national champions faced no competition on their domestic markets.

The increase in intra-EC FDI during the years 1987–90 could therefore be a result of companies anticipating genuinely new opportunities in markets that had previously been closed. This increase in intra-EC FDI coincides with the period when the single market programme began to be seen as credible by EC and non-EC investors alike. Although the Cockfield White Paper was produced in 1985 and the Single European Act ratified in 1986, the single market programme did not gather momentum until late 1987 and early 1988. The need for companies to invest on the basis of anticipated developments is all the more compelling when competitors have already moved to make such investments. Given the limited number of potential targets for acquisition, the companies that moved early had a better chance of increasing their market share and presence across the EC. This was particularly important in cases where there was no existing pan-European or international strength. As noted above, French companies were generally less international than EC rivals and they therefore sought to increase their European profile in advance of the Single Market.

Conclusions

This chapter has sought to address some of the policy and institutional factors which might affect intra-EC investment and to provide a qualitative assessment of their impact. All policies have some impact on investment; the task here is to make some judgments on their relative importance.[15] There does not seem to be much evidence that the levels of incentives (subsidies) help to explain FDI flows. Britain attracts a fair amount of intra-EC FDI but provides few subsidies; indeed it has the lowest level of subsidy. Although countries such as Portugal and Spain appear, at first sight, to have fairly high levels of aid, much of this has in fact gone into maintaining surplus capacity in specific sectors; this does not contribute much to attracting FDI. Some 75 per cent of the total aid provided to industry in the EC goes on support in the core areas, not the periphery, and there is a trend towards providing horizontal aid, e.g. for R&D or export funding.

There is at first sight a fairly good correlation between high levels of corporation tax in Germany and Denmark and low levels of inward FDI, suggesting that high taxes discourage FDI. The tax treatment of repatriated earnings is also not conducive to German investment. But it is important to consider the cumulative effect of incentives and tax treatment. High corporation tax in Germany goes hand in hand with a high level of investment tax incentives. On the other hand, low corporation tax in Britain is matched by an absence of tax incentives for investment. The figures also lend some support to the view that fairly favourable tax treatment in the Benelux countries helps to attract holding company operations, which may partly explain why other EC countries record extensive direct investment with those countries (especially in the form of financial investment in Luxembourg). On balance, therefore, tax treatment of cross-border investment seems to be a factor.

One area which has so far been scarcely touched by EC policies is that of structural impediments resulting from the legacies of past national regulatory policies which favoured national suppliers. These structural impediments are beginning to be eroded by national policies of privatization and liberalization, especially in Britain, and more recently by EC directives, most notably in the field of telecommunications. The fact that Britain moved furthest and fastest towards privatization could well be a factor behind higher levels of inward and outward FDI into Britain in those sectors.

The nexus of policy and structural issues affecting the role and importance of capital markets and the degree of openness of markets for corporate control seems to show the greatest correlation with patterns of investment. The most open corporate market, Britain, has the highest levels of FDI; the most closed market, at least for an economy of its size, Germany, has remarkably little inward FDI though increasing amounts of outward investment. France and Benelux, the other relatively open markets, also exhibit fairly high levels of FDI.

There is one important way, unrelated to specific directives or actions taken by DGIV, in which the Community has probably affected investment: by making credible the genuine liberalization of markets that had previously been closed by national policy or practice. The success of the internal market programme was not in passing a certain number of directives which had an immediate effect on barriers, but in generating the momentum which made the ultimate opening of markets credible. In order to ensure that they benefited from the new market opportunities, many firms moved to invest in other member states.

6

DIRECT INVESTMENT, EUROPEAN INTEGRATION AND COMPETITION POLICY

This study has had two objectives. The first has been to look at the extent to which information on direct investment in Europe provides any indication of a possible relocation of activities within the Single Market. The general conclusion is that, although variations in labour costs or differences in government regulation have resulted in some production being moved to more favourable locations, such shifts cannot possibly explain the tremendous flourishing of direct investment in Europe over the past few years. Most of this investment has occurred through acquisitions and has flowed mainly among the same group of countries and within the same industries.

To explain intra-European direct investment, we have stressed the importance of market proximity for firms, regardless of whether the market is the national, sub-regional or European one. Such a market-based strategy offers potentially enormous benefits to the European Community through its ability to spread competition within Europe far more effectively than trade alone could possibly achieve. We do not mean to imply that trade is no longer important; direct investment and trade are complements. The Community should therefore not only complete the Single Market programme but also consider what actions are required to facilitate market-based investment. At the same time, it should be vigilant against any potentially anti-competitive behaviour by investors. To achieve these objectives, the Commission should be armed with an activist competition policy.

Direct investment and economic integration: competition among firms

The various motives for FDI elucidated in Chapter 3 all focused on the efficiency gains from direct investment for the firms involved. Restructuring through mergers and acquisitions allows for greater economies of scale, while relocating production along the lines of comparative advantages in Europe offers potential factor cost savings. Market-based direct investment can be seen as a more efficient alternative to exporting if one assumes that information is an important input in the production process itself, enabling the firm to differentiate its output from that of competitors, and that this information is acquired more cheaply within the local market. Alternatively, one can focus on the potential for economies of scope or 'synergies' when market-based FDI involves the acquisition of a local firm. The target firm combines its distribution system and knowledge of the local market with the particular ownership advantage of the investor (technology, managerial skills, brand name or copyright, financial resources, etc.). As with any form of merger, these synergies may prove elusive. Porter (1987) has argued that the product diversification strategies of the 1960s were, for the most part, a failure. One can easily envisage similar difficulties in trying to merge two firms with very different corporate and national cultures.

Nevertheless, there are reasons to believe that the synergies from geographical diversification may be more tangible than those used to justify other merger strategies. As Davis (1990, p. 53) argues,

> While market entry is not, *per se*, a source of competitive advantage, it can unlock the value of the competitive advantages that either of the firms may have by enabling them to be extended to new markets. In this respect, the cross border mergers appear to be more firmly based on the existence of potential synergies than their domestic counterparts, when market entry is their goal, and it is at least not surprising that multinational diversity has a stronger link to profitability than product diversity.

Multinationality, in and of itself, can add little value to a firm if its various affiliates abroad are not competitive in each market in which they are located. Nevertheless, if Davis is right, market-based FDI is not just another form of diversification that will have to be undone in the future as firms retreat to 'core markets', much as they are now doing with product lines.

The gains from FDI are not just these static efficiency improvements. We have suggested in Chapter 3 that there are various market imperfections, such as culturally differentiated demand or the need for speed of delivery, which make trade difficult and thus shelter firms in national markets from the full brunt of international competition. Some of these barriers are erected by national governments and are now being attacked vigorously as part of the Single Market process. Other barriers are erected by local firms themselves, for instance through control of the local distribution network. Others are simply the natural result of geographical or cultural distance, which makes it difficult for firms to learn about opportunities abroad. We have argued in this book that simply removing non-tariff barriers will not necessarily make trade easier. Firms that are able may still prefer to locate directly. In these cases, direct investment in Europe makes intra-European competition more effective in bringing about the gains from integration.

Rather than simply greater efficiency, the real benefits from market-based investment are similar to those of intra-industry trade. Direct investment greatly expands the range of industries that must confront the full brunt of international competition. Krugman (1985, p. 41) has argued the same for intra-industry trade in a simple Cournot duopoly model. 'A new source of potential gains from trade is identified – namely, the effect of trade in increasing competition (and, if it induces exit, in "rationalising" production). More surprisingly, a new *cause* of trade is also identified: interpenetration of markets because oligopolists perceive a higher elasticity of demand on exports than on domestic sales.' In other words, because firms have a lower market share abroad, expanding in the foreign market appears to be a more fruitful endeavour than wresting a few more consumers away from competitors within their home market. What we have argued is that this strategy is as likely to be pursued through FDI as through trade.

The potential for greater competition through FDI than through trade can be seen most clearly with respect to American investment in Europe. A large proportion of American exports to Europe is through US MNEs, and for many of these firms their local production in Europe greatly exceeds any exports from home. The competition that EC firms face from their American rivals is therefore much more likely to come from FDI than from trade. The same will no doubt soon be true for Japanese firms. Not only is trade of secondary importance for many US MNEs, but the effect of US competition is also likely to be greater than that indicated simply by the level of sales in Europe. What is equally important is the *distribution* of that investment. Many US MNEs are effectively pan-European in the sense that they are represented in each major market within Europe. In contrast, many of their rivals are strongly dependent on their own national markets, e.g. automobiles and computers. Through this pan-European presence, these US firms may already have avoided some, though by no means all, of the potential barriers to conducting business within Europe.

The effect of these pan-European firms on competition within the Community will vary according to the circumstances, but clearly in the absence of collusive or predatory behaviour on their part, competition is likely to increase. The Cecchini Report (1988) looks at the industries with the worst barriers and estimates their costs in terms of economic welfare. The authors do not look sufficiently at the reasons why other sectors are less afflicted by similar barriers. For example, in spite of public procurement practices in the mainframe computer industry, the sector is considered to be highly competitive 'even if it is largely characterised by indigenous producers competing against IBM in each national market' (p. 22). We would argue instead that the sector faces competition *precisely because IBM has invested directly in each major market*. By creating subsidiaries in several national markets, IBM has been able to circumvent some of the favouritism in government procurement in those markets towards local firms. Similar examples can be found in all sectors characterized by public purchasing of capital equipment. In each case, the presence of an outsider has stimulated competition and tended to break down the established structure.

For American MNEs, the sheer volume of local sales compared with exports speaks to the importance of direct investment as a source of competition. Does market-based FDI play a similar role within the Community? Unfortunately, we have very little information about the sales levels of European affiliates in other member states. Sales of German MNEs through their affiliates in the rest of the EC are almost identical to German exports to those countries. Sales by affiliates of German firms in Spain, Austria, the UK and France are all higher than German exports to those countries. Following the sweeping changes in ownership across Europe in the 1980s, the level of sales relative to exports must have increased dramatically for all major outward investors.

These gains are not necessarily contingent on the establishment of new plants. Even when FDI occurs through acquisitions, there may be large gains from upsetting the competitive status quo in the host market. *The Financial Times* suggested that the main benefit from the takeover of

Midland Bank by the Hong Kong and Shanghai Banking Corporation was the intensification of competition within the British banking sector because of the strong balance-sheet backing that HSBC would provide to Midland.[1]

The Cecchini Report (1988, p. 84), in discussing the benefits of the Single Market, devoted surprisingly little attention to the potential for enhancing competition. The gains from exploiting economies of scale more fully (61 billion ecus) exceeded those from intensified competition reducing business inefficiencies and monopoly profits (46 billion ecus). The aim of the Single Market is not just improved consumer welfare, it is also to make European firms more innovative and hence more competitive on world markets. The chief means of making EC firms more innovative, according to the Commission, is not through the creation of a larger market but rather from the increase in competition. 'Market size does not, as such, have a significant effect on innovation ... The beneficial effects of European integration on innovation derive more from the intensification of competition than from phenomena linked to size' (*European Economy*, 1988, p. 128).

Direct investment and political integration: competition among rules

Direct investment not only makes firms compete more, it also makes governments monitor and sometimes imitate policies in the rest of Europe. All policies have a potential effect on the attractiveness of a country as a location for firms' various activities. Cases can be found of firms relocating in response to any particular policy. And governments routinely invoke the need to remain attractive as a location as a reason for rejecting some policy initiative, often from Brussels. Governments also compete vigorously through incentives to attract mobile investors.

Our analysis of investment patterns within Europe has suggested that, in spite of the perception of governments that their policies have a strong impact on FDI flows, the role of policies is often greatly exaggerated. Firms are not so much engaging in regulatory arbitrage as responding to the competitors' actions by pushing into foreign markets. When firms do relocate production from one country to another, it is more likely to be because of the desire for market proximity than from any preference for one regulatory environment over another. Our analysis has focused broadly on horizontal policies. As one gets down into specific sectors, the effects of regulatory arbitrage are more likely to be discernible.

One reason why policies were not found to have a strong overall impact on direct investment may be because it is very difficult to pick up the compound effects of policies. It is conceivable that the positive effects of one policy are neutralized by the negative effects of another and vice versa. Thus the relatively high levels of subsidization in Germany may be a way of compensating for other factors, such as a generally fairly high level of regulation of the economy. This might go some way to explaining why Germany provides a relatively high level of subsidies but still does not attract a lot of inward FDI. It also means that effective policy coordination and fine-tuning may yet have an effect on investment flows. The same arguments can be made if we look only at investment incentives targeted towards footloose firms. Information on American investment abroad has shown that investment incentives are routinely coupled with performance requirements which by themselves serve to discourage investors.

If there is only a marginal impact from policies there is no strong case for radical changes, at least in horizontal national policies such as social and tax policies, in order to bring them in line with those elsewhere in the Community for fear of discouraging investment. In the medium term, it appears that the Single Market can accommodate a fairly wide diversity in regulatory regimes in Europe. Competition among rules is a very slow process. In the long run, such competition will be felt primarily through the effect of policies on the appeal of various national markets or market clusters within Europe. Vibrant and growing markets will attract the most investment, creating a situation in which the virtuous are rewarded disproportionately.

One area in which we did find some correlation between investment flows and policy was in that group of policies which affect the size and structure of the capital markets in the EC. A large, open capital market seems to promote both inward and outward investment, and there are obvious reasons why this might be so. Capital markets facilitate take-overs in that country as well as providing a source of funds for domestic firms to expand abroad. Thus any policies, such as financial market regulation or the rules pertaining to stock exchanges, which enhance the growth of capital markets could well stimulate investment. Unlike with other policy variables, however, the capital market structure of a country is the result of a set of policies, or even practices of market operators, rather than any specific policy. These policies are, in turn, intimately linked with the form of market economy that exists in each country. Rather than regulatory arbitrage between discrete policies in different countries, the competition is between countries with different approaches to the regulation of capital markets and to how industry is financed. The most clear-cut differences, as discussed in Chapter 5, are those between the Anglo-Saxon and German approaches, the former being associated with higher levels of cross-border investment. In this case competition among rules is more of a competition among systems.

Such systemic competition is healthy for the European economy, and we make no presumption about whether the Anglo-Saxon or continental system is superior. At the same time, if market-based FDI stimulates competition and if most of this investment occurs through mergers and acquisitions, there is a case for removing the barriers to takeovers within the EC by adopting the company law provisions in the Single Market programme, notably the Second, Fifth and Thirteenth Company Law Directives. These directives remove the more blatant legal barriers to takeovers in member states. The Second Company Law Directive, for example, precludes the purchase of a parent company's shares by a subsidiary, a device used as a defence against hostile takeovers. The Fifth Company Law Directive removes barriers to takeover in the shape of limits on voting rights, while the Thirteenth establishes a code on takeovers equivalent to that guaranteed by the British Takeover Panel.

Progress on these directives has been blocked by differences among the member states on the appropriate company structure, including differences over the role of codetermination. Paradoxically the British government has included this set of directives as candidates for removal from Community competence as part of the subsidiarity exercise.[2] Even if the more immediate barriers to takeover were to be removed, however, there would remain the fundamental differences in the structure and operation of the various capital markets, with convergence most likely to occur through systemic competition.

Another area where policy coordination could prove beneficial is in terms of tax treatment where there is a clear bias against cross-border investment as opposed to investment within each member state. As suggested in the Ruding Committee and by a number of surveys of business opinion, this bias should be removed even if there is no need to harmonize the rates of corporation tax across the EC because it will facilitate market-based direct investment and thus promote competition. As the European Commission has proposed, this should be done by legislation to bring the tax treatment of subsidiaries in other EC member states in line with that in the home country.

In the field of subsidies the study suggests that these have no proven effect on the overall pattern of investment flows, even if they may have some marginal effects with regard to specific projects. If the project concerned is a significant investment, such marginal effects could well be of considerable importance to a local community or region in desperate need of investment and jobs. Nevertheless this study provides further evidence for the view that subsidies tend to favour the investing company most, since they are provided by regional or local governments in the belief that a subsidy is needed to attract the firm, when in most cases firms base their investment decision primarily on other factors.

Government policies are both general and specific, and the one most obviously designed to alter location decisions is the use of investment incentives. Virtually all countries, including even Cuba and North Korea, encourage MNEs to locate production within their economy. In Europe, the competition is particularly acute because as the market becomes more integrated firms will supposedly become less particular about where they locate. The same competition characterizes FDI in the US although it is at a state level. Some authors such as Reich (1991) have even gone so far as to suggest that this competition now takes place at a global level. Focusing on the highest value-added activities, Reich argues that 'the location of headquarters is not a matter of great importance; it is not even necessarily in the country where most of the company's shareholders or employees are' (p. 80). His policy recommendation for an era of global companies is that 'in a world in which every other nation is bidding for high value-added jobs, America must negotiate as well' (p. 84).

This is precisely the danger of competitive bidding that is likely to arise when firms are perceived to be footloose. Evidence from direct investment in Europe suggests that such is not the case in many industries although incentives may divert investment away from other members of a cluster. Overall, incentives are not likely to influence the vast bulk of investment flows, whether in Europe or globally. What they do instead is to transfer more of the gain from inward investment to the investing firm and away from the host country. Incentives may also distort the type of investment that a country receives. The example of Ireland demonstrates how subsidies can promote capital-intensive production in a relatively labour-abundant country, leading to what the OECD (1985, p. 43) terms a 'dual economy' with little interaction between foreign and indigenous sectors.

Arguments relating to such export platform investments as we described in Ireland and Portugal have typically been voiced in the context of the developing world. Studies of investment in developing countries such as Lim and Pang (1991) have shown that export platforms have fewer links with the local economy than investment oriented to the local market. Too often, countries lure foreign MNEs as a way of compensating for their own inability to stimulate indigenous enterprise. Whatever one hopes to gain from inward investment, whether capital, employment, technology or exports, studies have repeatedly demonstrated that it can only serve to complement domestic initiatives in the same area.[3] Ireland may have over 40 per cent of its manufacturing employment in foreign-owned firms but it still has the highest unemployment levels in Europe. Ford and IBM may be among the top five exporters from Britain, along with dozens of other foreign firms that export extensively, but they have done little to erode persistent British trade deficits. We are not suggesting that investors should be gauged in this way. They contribute in myriad ways to the national economy in which they locate, but by themselves they can do little to alter the fundamental economic situation in each country. By offering generous incentives, governments limit resources available to strengthen the productivity of the nation as a whole through training and infrastructure improvements, and the like.

A strong case can be made for some sort of control on incentives by host governments. It is all the more compelling when, as Chapter 5 showed, most of the aid is in fact finding its way to firms in the relatively wealthy core of the EC rather than to the peripheral regions, where it might be needed to compensate for less favourable economic conditions. Not only are incentives unlikely to be effective given that other countries offer similar inducements, but they are also likely to limit the potential benefit to the host country from that investment. The problem is that any control would conflict both with regional policies in host countries and with the division of powers between national governments and the regional authorities within the country. In spite of these difficulties, the Commission has gone farther in containing competitive bidding than has been done at a multilateral level. In the automobile sector, the Commission recently required the Austrian government to take back some of the subsidy it had offered to a joint venture between a local company and Chrysler.

We are not suggesting that there should be no mechanism for ensuring that depressed areas can enhance their appeal to firms. The British and French governments, though not the Spanish one, have been successful in channelling Japanese factories into areas that have witnessed a dramatic decline of their own industries such as shipbuilding. If these policies can be justified at a national level they can also be used at a regional one. We are arguing instead that such policies would be more effective if there were more controls on incentives offered by the richest markets. Furthermore, these incentives should be tailored so as to enhance the natural advantages of each location. Unfortunately, economic recession and continued opposition to Commission intervention could mean that the Commission will continue to face political constraints on the use of its legal powers.

This is also the case with regard to the application of Article 90 (EEC) to control public enterprise and to open the markets which have long been dominated by public monopoly operators. Article 90 has always been applicable to such sectors, or so the Commission has argued, with some support from the European Court of Justice, but it has never been applied because of political opposition to Commission intervention.

Our brief examination of regulated sectors, such as the public services, suggests that much more work is needed in this area. There could well be some correlation between privatization and an increase in inward and outward investment flows, as in Britain. If market-based investment is to be allowed to play an active role in introducing competition throughout the internal market, there must be continued efforts to open these sectors to investment. The Commission has made some progress in using the Article 90 (EEC) provisions, which cover public enterprise, but there is undoubtedly a case for doing more.

Our analysis has deliberately been conducted at a high level of aggregation. In certain industries, policy divergences in one particular area may loom exceptionally large in the investment decision. We saw in Chapter 3 that policy differences, principally relating to taxation, have caused massive recorded inflows into the Benelux countries in the banking sector. Other sectors may also be swayed by similar considerations. Case-studies would have revealed certain instances of firms driven abroad by lower taxes, for example, but they would have provided little evidence of the *relative* importance of such factors across the full gamut of European industry. It is the relative importance of each variable that is of interest to us because it helps us to understand where direct investment brings the greatest pressure to bear on both firms and governments within the Single Market.

Our scepticism concerning the influence of policies on direct investment is based on the strong assumption that much of the cross-border investment that we observe in Europe is for the purposes of effective market access and does not constitute a reallocation of resources throughout Europe. Such market-based investment poses far greater risks and offers potentially far greater rewards than other investments based strictly on cost considerations. Our major policy recommendations will concentrate on market-based FDI. How can governments minimize the risks of collusion and monopolistic behaviour by firms while at the same time enhancing the potential gains that such investment can offer in terms of greater competition? In both cases there is a need for an active competition policy pursued both by the Commission and by national governments.

The need for an active competition policy

The potential gains from direct investment may greatly exceed those expected from trade by spreading competition more effectively throughout the Community. But there are also risks. By reducing the number of competitors, acquisitions also potentially reduce the level of competition, although the relationship need by no means be one to one. Indeed, the elimination of competition may sometimes be the sole purpose of the acquirer. Chandler (1990, p. 424) has suggested that the fact that earlier merger waves in the late nineteenth and early twentieth century involved British and American firms more than German ones is due mostly to the fact that cartels were permitted in Germany at that time but not in the Anglo-Saxon countries. The only alternative open to those firms in the face of 'ruinous competition' was to merge with their rivals. Efficiency considerations are not the only reason why firms acquire rivals. It is not too far-fetched to describe some industries as oligopolies in search of a monopoly. We make no presumption that firms act competitively of their own free will. Some do, but others do not. If we have not emphasized the darker side of oligopolistic behaviour it is because we feel that competition policy – if applied with conviction at both a regional and a national level – can be adequate to the task of restraining such anti-competitive behaviour.

The increase in cross-border mergers and acquisitions has certainly increased the potential for competition by breaking down established national champion or oligopolistic structures. In this sense market-based FDI is aggressive and likely to contribute to competition. The need now for the European Community is to ensure that this initial competitive impulse does not eventually create a European oligopoly in place of national ones. Competition policy is essential in this regard. The EC has a range of policy instruments available in the field of competition policy which will have to be refined to ensure that a flexible but effective regulation of competition occurs at the European level. Competition policy will also have to be coordinated with commercial policy on both trade and investment from outside the Community and with regulatory policies in sectors such as pharmaceuticals, transport, energy, telecommunications or financial services, where the issue of the public good is vital.

The Community has developed a consistent and coherent policy towards restrictive business practices, cartels and the abuse of market dominance. The Treaty of Rome provides the EC with competence in this area through Articles 85 and 86 (EEC). Through a combination of Commission initiatives and ECJ rulings these treaty provisions have been developed and adapted to the requirements of the market. The body of Community law and practice that has evolved over a thirty-year period has also been adopted by the member states so that national and Community approaches are broadly consistent.

In a number of notable cases, such as the Continental Can case in 1972 and the Philip Morris case in 1987, the ECJ has ruled that Articles 85 and 86 (EEC) can be used, in certain circumstances, to stop mergers or acquisitions. Normally these articles can act only to prohibit or regulate the actions of existing companies and not to influence the structure of a given sector. But these treaty provisions can be used to block mergers when restrictive practices or market dominance are used to bring about a merger. The decisions of the Court in these cases have served as a catalyst for efforts to create an EC merger control instrument.

The merger control regulation which was adopted in December 1989 constitutes the key instrument available to the European Commission in any policy aimed at ensuring that cross-border mergers or acquisitions do not result in Europe-wide oligopolies against the consumer or general interest. How this instrument is used will have a considerable impact on whether or not the new industrial structures that are emerging from cross-border investment are competitive.

Agreement on the merger regulation was delayed for some 15 years by a controversy over the objectives of EC policy. Should this be competition-based or should it also pursue industrial policy objectives by, for example, considering the impact of any merger on the competitive position of the affected industry in Europe vis-à-vis the rest of the world? This controversy has pitted the competition-minded Germans and Dutch, later joined by the British, against the industrial policy-minded French and Italians. The letter of the 1989 regulation came down squarely on the side of competition policy. Indeed, Woolcock (1990) has argued that the text is more narrowly competition-based than Articles 85 and 86 (EEC).

The real test of the regulation is how it is applied. To date some 60–70 cases have been considered by the Commission, and only once has it blocked a merger: the takeover of De Havilland by Aérospatiale in late 1991. The decision was controversial in France because the French authorities stressed the industrial logic of the merger, but the Commission remained firm. Although other mergers have been modified in order to satisfy Commission concerns, this remains the only case of the Commission blocking a cross-border merger.

The use of the merger control regulation is likely to continue to divide those favouring competition-based and industrial policy approaches, with no consensus emerging for quite some time. After all, it took a couple of decades in the case of EC policy on cartels. This schism, together with opposition to the degree of central control which an active EC competition inevitably implies, will make any Commission endeavours difficult. Fears of centralization tendencies in the EC are being used by those who oppose an active EC competition policy, making it all the more necessary to articulate the case for a strong, coherent EC competition policy. Such a policy is entirely consistent with any reasonable definition of subsidiarity because national competition authorities are simply not in a position to ensure effective competition on an EC-wide basis.

Outstanding issues concerning the operation of the merger control regulation include the question of its application to what is termed dual dominance in which, rather than merging to create a dominant company, two companies effectively divide the market between them in an attempt to avoid an EC action under the regulation. In the recent Perrier case in 1992 the Commission argued that a merger which does not necessarily clash with the provisions of the merger control regulation by establishing a dominant market position can still be opposed if it creates joint dominance of the market. The Commission forced the companies concerned to sell a number of products to a third competitor. The application of the merger control regulation in such cases could prove to be of central importance because many of the cross-border mergers and acquisitions are in fact agreements between established producers in which they exchange a number of product lines in order to consolidate their positions in different markets across the EC. Such *accords cadres* could reduce rather than increase competition.

The competence of the Commission can be extended by lowering the threshold for turnover of the two companies, thus expanding the coverage of the regulation. The threshold for global turnover was set at 5 billion ecus in the 1989 regulation, but there is provision for a review in 1993.

The most challenging task for EC policy is to achieve a proper balance between ensuring sufficient flexibility to enable a merger control policy to be effective and limiting the use of EC-level merger control as an instrument of industrial policy. The Commission has been criticized for being both judge and jury in competition policy cases because it not only carries out the technical analysis of the impact of any merger on market structure and behaviour but also decides on whether the merger should be permitted. Under the German system of merger controls these two functions are separated between the Federal Cartel Office, which assesses the effects on competition, and the Ministry of Economics, which determines whether other factors override competition considerations. This approach provides flexibility whilst ensuring that any discretion used is at least transparent. A similar model has been proposed for the EC by Hölzer (1990). There are a number of possible options available. For example, an independent competition body (European Cartel Office) could be established, and would pass its judgment to the Commission. Alternatively the Commission could continue with the task of making the assessment on competition grounds but pass on the final decision to the Council of Ministers.

It is not the place here to argue the merits of these various possible developments of EC merger control policy. The point we wish to make is that these questions must be addressed sooner rather than later. The convergence of national policies and the Community policy on cartels took a couple of decades. It must be done more quickly for merger controls because the current cross-border FDI is creating structures which, once established, will be difficult to change. To wait for a common policy to emerge is to abdicate responsibility for how Europe-wide oligopolistic competition is to take place.

Competition policy should be more than just reactive. The Commission must initiate measures to open up the closed sectors discussed in Chapter 5. The European Commission has used the competition provisions of the treaty (Article 90 EEC) to do this in the case of telecommunications, and its interpretations were supported by the European Court of Justice. While the Commission may have been successful in the telecommunications sector, the cases of electricity and gas have shown there are political limits to how far the Commission can go. Factors other than free flows of FDI and competition will have to be sorted out first. For example, how should these sectors, which many countries consider to be natural monopolies and therefore legitimate objects of public regulation, be regulated at a European level? Nevertheless, as the telecommunications case has shown, the threat of using Article 90 (EEC) can be effective in forcing the member states to make serious efforts to find agreed solutions to common regulatory policy issues. This in turn greatly enhances the scope for competition in the European market, much of which, we have argued in this book, will come from FDI.

Last but by no means least it must be remembered that a good deal of the competition through direct investment in Europe has come from US and, more recently, Japanese firms. Commercial policy with respect to trade and investment must therefore be combined with competition policy in order to ensure that the European market is genuinely competitive. Any discussion of the contribution that trade policy can make to competition within the EC inevitably involves the question of the role of competition policy in international competitiveness, i.e. whether it is possible to allow for less competition on the EC market because of import competition. It is at this point that one begins to run up against the limits of competition policy at an EC level. All competition policies must start from a definition of the relevant market. The integration of the European economy means that in more and more cases the relevant market is no longer national but rather encompasses neighbouring countries, the whole of Europe or even the world market. When the market is global, it becomes doubtful whether even European competition policy is adequate or whether instead there is not a need for either a global competition policy or some coordination or approximation of European, US and Japanese policies.

Conclusion

Direct investment is a potent force behind European integration, bringing firms and ultimately governments into more direct competition. In this study we have described how firms' strategies interact with the political and economic processes of integration. This interaction is still poorly understood, as direct investment by European firms in their own region is, by and large, only a recent phenomenon. Our analysis suggests that such investment is in many ways similar to intra-European trade. It not only follows a similar pattern characterized by market clusters but it also often flows back and forth on an intra-industry basis. We refer to such investment as market-based.

Greater integration is not inconsistent with an expansion of market-based investment. We argued in Chapter 3 that distance costs are likely to remain important even as barriers to trade are removed. Indeed, to the extent that the Single Market makes competition in each national market more intense, it will lead to increased pressure for firms to establish a local presence within major markets or market clusters. When such market access is constrained by structural impediments in the host country, then the process of European integration itself is slowed down, just as it is with barriers to trade. For this reason, the Commission needs to look at the various barriers to trade and investment mentioned in Chapter 5 as coterminous obstacles in the path of the Single Market.

Not all investment in Europe is market-based. The peripheral countries have received some sizeable investments partly in search of lower labour costs, and these investments may well help to accelerate the process of economic convergence within Europe, but while inward investment may often be useful, it is not sufficient by itself to bring about this convergence.

The same caution should be exercised with respect to a possible convergence of policies through regulatory arbitrage orchestrated by MNEs. Government ministers, trade union officials and employer associations routinely invoke the effect of policies on the attractiveness of their economy as a location for investment. Their claims often greatly exaggerate the importance of specific policies on firms' investment decisions. Direct investment is driven by a complex assessment of dozens of factors, and it is unlikely that the difference of a few percentage points in wage or tax rates will cause a massive relocation of economic activity in Europe. Ultimately there will be winners and losers from competition among rules, but such competition is a long-term phenomenon. In the meantime, there appears to be ample scope for diversity of policies even within the Single Market. It is the whole spectrum of policies that a government selects, together with their effect on that particular market, that matters for investors.

To create a genuine Single Market and to derive the greatest benefits from further integration, the policy challenge for Europe in the 1990s is to maximize competition among firms through activist policies to remove impediments to both trade and investment and to discourage collusive behaviour while at the same time keeping a firm rein on the competition among governments for mobile investment.

APPENDIX:
THE DETERMINANTS OF
THE PATTERN OF
INVESTMENT IN EUROPE

Chapter 4 described patterns of direct investment in Europe, noting that large and neighbouring markets are often favoured by investors. Some evidence was also provided of firms shifting labour-intensive operations to the periphery of Europe. Throughout this book, we have tended to look at the behaviour of firms at a highly aggregated level, not because we think all industries are the same, but because we are interested in the relative importance of each factor behind the growth of direct investment in Europe. Because different motives for FDI imply different outcomes in terms of European integration, the relative significance of each type of investment provides clues to the future shape of the Community and to the path that will lead us there. The analysis in Chapter 4 did not permit us satisfactorily to assign different weights to each variable. For that we need to use econometric analysis, which separates the variables and measures their effects individually. This Appendix presents two equations for intra-European direct investment (IEDI) which contain all of the variables that appeared in Chapters 3 and 4.

Direct investment does not lend itself very easily to hypothesis testing for the simple reason that the economic literature on the subject is so eclectic. This eclecticism is the natural outcome of the wide diversity of motives that might lead a firm to invest abroad, some of which were described in Chapter 3. Because of this diversity, tests of the determinants of FDI have tended to take similar forms, regardless of the implied hypothesis of the authors. These tests are loosely based on a gravity model formulation, along with some variable to capture labour cost differences to account for the fact that, in theory, capital should flow to capital-scarce locations. We use per capita income in each host country as a rough proxy for relative factor endowments. Gravity models have also been extremely successful in explaining existing trade patterns, not only within Europe but worldwide.

Gravity models usually take the following functional form:

$$PX_{ij} = \beta_0 (Y_i)^{\beta 1} (Y_j)^{\beta 2} (D_{ij})^{\beta 3} (A_{ij})^{\beta 4} u_{ij}$$

where PX_{ij} is the nominal value of the flow in question, Y_i and Y_j are the nominal GNP of the two countries, D_{ij} is the distance between the two countries, and A_{ij} is a vector of possible explanatory variables which either aid or obstruct the flow between the two countries. Balassa and Bauwens (1988) use a similar form to estimate the share of trade between European countries that is intra-industry. They include various host country variables such as GDP per capita, GDP, differences in economic size and wealth between the two countries, geographical distance, and several dummy variables such as common borders, participation in the EC or EFTA, and a common language. They find that geographical and cultural factors such as distance, borders and a common language are more significant than participation in the EC in explaining both the importance of intra-industry trade and the pattern of overall trade.

Gravity models have been widely criticized, notably for their lack of any clear underlying model behind the reduced form equation. Nevertheless, a gravity model of direct investment in Europe provides insights into the location choices of firms from different countries even if it does not tell us why firms have made such choices. Our model estimated here provides further evidence of the various strategies described in Figure 3.2.

Tests of intra-European direct investment are rare. Molle and Morsink (1991) and Culem (1988) both try to determine the pattern of IEDI based on annual flows. We use stock figures instead, both because they are often more complete and less volatile and because flows of investment represent merely an adjustment towards an equilibrium, not the equilibrium itself.

Our test of IEDI will take the following logarithmic form:

$$LFDI = \beta_0 + \beta_1 LY_a + \beta_2 LY_b + \beta_3 D + \beta 4 EC + \beta_{5-7} DHost + \beta_{8-14} DHome$$

All variables beginning with L are expressed in logarithmic form based on a common currency.

LFDI: stock of direct investment in the rest of Europe for each of the following home countries: UK, Germany, Italy, France, Netherlands, Sweden, Denmark, Spain

Table A.1 The determinants of the pattern of FDI in Europe

Variable	Coefficient	T-ratio
Equation 1		
Intercept	-25.2	-1.4
LY_a	3.0	2.6
LY_b	1.3	6.7
LYP_b	-1.7	-2.1
LD	-2.1	-5.6
DHost:		
Switzerland	2.7	3.4
Netherlands	2.2	2.7
Luxembourg	6.2	3.7
DHome:		
France	-1.2	-1.5
Germany	-0.8	-0.9
Italy	-2.1	-2.7
Netherlands	3.5	2.5
UK	0.6	0.7
Sweden	3.6	2.0
Denmark	4.5	1.9

Observations: 119
R^2 (adj.) = 0.61
Durbin-Watson = 2.22

Equation 2		
Intercept	-38.3	-2.0
LY_a	3.2	2.8
LY_b	1.1	4.8
LYP_b	-0.5	-0.5
LD	-1.9	-4.8
EC	1.2	2.0

DHost and DHome do not change significantly from Equation 1 and are not shown here.

Observations: 119
R^2 (adj.) = 0.59
Durbin-Watson = 2.03

LY_a: GNP (current dollars and purchasing power parities) of home country

LY_b: GNP (current dollars and PPPs) of host country

LYP_b: Per capita GNP of host country (current dollars and PPPs)

LD: Distance between capital cities (Frankfurt for Germany)

EC: Dummy to reflect EC membership of host country

DHost: Dummies to reflect the importance of certain locations as financial centres (Luxembourg, Netherlands, Switzerland) which exaggerates their importance in terms of FDI flows.

DHome: Dummies to allow for intercept shifts among the various home countries

LFDI is the stock of direct investment in other European countries by eight different home countries in Europe, yielding 119 observations, all expressed in a common currency. In other words, we look at how much French or German firms, for example, have invested in other European countries. To compensate for the fact that different home countries invest different levels abroad, we have included dummies for each home country. Technically, these dummy variables allow the intercept terms to differ across countries, although the slope is constrained to remain constant across home countries on the assumption that the variables in our equations affect investors in much the same way, regardless of their country of origin. This latter assumption may naturally be questioned, but when we ran regressions for individual home countries (not shown here) the same variables were significant in all cases, so the problems introduced by this constraint should not be exaggerated.

The results are presented in Table A.1. The variables of most interest to us are those expressed in logarithmic form, as well as the dummy to reflect EC membership. The results conform to those typically found for gravity models of both trade and investment. Larger economies generally invest more abroad, as we discussed in Chapter 2. Because we are mostly interested in the location rather than the origin of investment, the home country market size variable LY_a, together with the individual home country dummies, mostly serve to remove this home country effect on the level of flows.

So where do firms invest within Europe? In Equation 1, all variables are significant, but not equally so. As we can see from the T-ratios which give us an idea of the explanatory strength of each variable, host country market size followed by physical distance are the most significant. Lower labour costs, as proxied by per capita income, also appeal to firms, but the variable is much less significant in Equation 1 and insignificant in Equation 2.

Equation 2 includes a dummy variable to capture whether a particular host country is a member of the EC on the assumption that a country increases its appeal as a location when it participates in the Community. Chapter 4 provided examples of peripheral countries that have substantially increased inflows into their country in the years immediately following EC membership. Equation 2 suggests that this is indeed the case, but at the same time, per capita income becomes insignificant, suggesting that it is not the labour cost elements behind this greater inflow that matter. Unfortunately, the EC variable is closely related to the other variables since the only non-EC countries are all small, rich and often on the periphery of Europe, thus making it difficult to separate the various influences. In other specifications of the model the EC variable was not significant, just as Balassa and Bauwens (1988) found for European trade flows.

The only two variables which are consistently and strongly significant determinants of where firms invest in Europe are those of host country market size and distance. We can only conclude from this that, in relative terms, they have the greatest influence on firms' behaviour in Europe. The same two appeared significant for American and Japanese investment in Europe (not shown here), where distance was taken to mean distance from the centre of Europe (Brussels). These results strengthen our arguments in Chapters 3 and 4 that firms are often interested in gaining access to other geographical markets within Europe when they invest, and that they are often constrained by distances. As we stressed in those chapters, the importance of market size should not be construed as a failure of integration, since firms seem to prefer to congregate in areas of high demand even in homogeneous markets like the United States. Nevertheless, the distance variable does appear to impose a constraint on firms that more favourable wage costs or policies in some other corner of Europe are not strong enough to overcome.

NOTES

Chapter 1: Introduction

1 Direct investment is defined as 'an investment that is made to acquire a lasting interest in an enterprise operating in an economy other than that of the investor, the investor's purpose being to have an effective voice in the management of the enterprise' (IMF, 1977).

2 Michael Cassell, 'Euro doubts put inward investment under threat', *The Financial Times*, 20 October 1992.

Chapter 2: Trends in direct investment in Europe

1 The Dutch investments may also be partly British as they include the Anglo-Dutch companies Royal Dutch/Shell and Unilever.

2 One such call was made by Dr Toyoda, President of Toyota, at a meeting of the UK–Japan 2000 Group in March 1989.

3 Forsgren et al. (1992) estimate that Electrolux alone accounts for one-third of the employment of Swedish firms abroad.

4 One reason for this discrepancy may be that the retained earnings of existing affiliates are not adequately captured in the Bundesbank figures, though they are included in the German definition of FDI.

Chapter 3: Motives for direct investment in Europe

1 Guy de Jonquières and William Dawkins, 'An appetite for acquisitions', *The Financial Times*, 27 January 1992.

2 For a similar, more recent observation, see *European Economy*, 1990, p. 68.

3 Guy de Jonquières and William Dawkins, 'An appetite for acquisitions'.

4 Paul Abrahams, 'Spotlight shines on Rhône–Poulenc', *The Financial Times*, 10 March 1992.

5 I.H. Fazey, 'Pilkington shatters 165 years of history', *The Financial Times*, 9 October 1991.

6 Charles Leadbeater, 'Du Pont stretches its European strategy', *The Financial Times*, 9 August 1991.

Chapter 4: European integration, trade and investment patterns

1 Kieran Cooke, 'Irish exporters fear being made Europe's passenger', *The Financial Times*, 18 January 1990.
2 Peter Wise, 'Lowest wages and fewest strikes', *The Financial Times*, 30 April 1990.
3 David Gardner, 'Auto giants point the way', *The Financial Times*, 4 November 1991.

Chapter 5: Governments and firms

1 See Commission of the European Communities (1992b) for the latest survey results.
2 Much of the rest of aid goes to coal mining and transport (mainly to rail). Aid for transport varies dramatically from 20 per cent of value added in Belgium (1988–90) to 1.2 per cent in Italy and Spain. Such aid may affect the level of infrastructure and hence investment.
3 See Council Resolution on 'A framework of the systems of regional aid', *Official Journal*, C111, 1971. For this and all texts see Commission of the European Communities, *Competition Law in the European Communities*, vol. II: 'Rules applicable to state aids', Brussels, 1990.
4 See 'Community framework on state aids for research and development', *Official Journal*, C83, 1986.
5 See Commission of the European Communities, *First Survey on State Aids in the European Community*, Luxembourg, 1989. The third survey was produced in July 1992.
6 See Commission of the European Communities, *Twentieth Report on Competition Policy*, Luxembourg, 1991, p. 157.
7 See Commission Directive 80/723/EEC, *Official Journal*, L195, 29 July 1980. OECD work suggests that the main use of equity injections is, as one would expect, in the form of sectoral aid for nationalized or mixed ownership companies facing bankruptcy.
8 See Commission communication to the member states, *Official Journal*, C273, 1991.
9 See the annual *Reports on Competition Policy* by the European Commission on individual cases.
10 One interesting development has been the proposal by the current Swedish government that companies should be obliged to remove provisions in their articles of association which limit voting rights on other measures which form impediments to takeover.
11 See *M&A Europe*, January/February 1992 and previous years. The European Commission's *Twentieth Report on Competition Policy* also

provides a matrix indicating similar trends.

12 See OECD (1992b).

13 See OECD (1992b), pp. 83–100.

14 See OECD (1992b) for details of the electricity, gas, oil and transport sectors.

15 An analogous exercise was carried out by the OECD and the negotiators in the GATT talks on trade-related investment measures (TRIMs) during the Uruguay round negotiations in 1988–90. In the case of the GATT negotiations the focus was on local content provisions, import and export performance requirements, licensing etc., all of which are prohibited within the EC. Many of the policy variables discussed here are of course subject to other GATT provisions, e.g. the subsidies code, regulatory barriers in telecommunications (GATS negotiations), or are moving onto the GATT agenda (competition policy).

Chapter 6: Direct investment, European integration and competition policy

1 'From here to Hong Kong', *The Financial Times*, 18 March 1992.

2 See *Agence Europe*, 7 December 1992.

3 See, for example, the discussion in World Bank (1991), notably Chapter 5 on 'Integration with the global economy'.

REFERENCES

Balassa, Bela, and Luc Bauwens (1988), 'The determinants of intra-European trade in manufactured goods', *European Economic Review*, 32.

Bliss, Christopher, and Jorge Braga de Macedo (1990), *Unity with Diversity in the European Economy: The Community's Southern Frontier*, Centre for Economic Policy Research/Cambridge University Press, Cambridge.

Cantwell, John (1992a), 'The effects of integration on the structure of multinational corporation activity in the EC', in M. Klein and P. Welfens (eds), *Multinationals in the New Europe and Global Trade*, Springer Verlag, Berlin.

Cantwell, John (1992b), *Multinational Investment in Modern Europe: Strategic Interaction in the Integrated Community*, Edward Elgar, Aldershot, Hants.

Cantwell, John, and Francesca Sanna Randaccio (1992), 'Intra-industry direct investment in the European Community: oligopolistic rivalry and technological competition', in J. Cantwell (ed.), *Multinational Investment in Modern Europe*, Edward Elgar, Aldershot, Hants.

Caves, Richard (1971), 'Industrial corporations: The industrial economics of foreign investment', *Economica*, February.

Cecchini, Paolo, et al. (1988), *The European Challenge: The Benefits of a Single Market*, translated by John Robinson, Wildwood House, Aldershot, Hants.

Chandler, Alfred (1990), *Scale and Scope: The Dynamics of Industrial Capitalism*, Harvard University Press, London.

Commission of the European Communities (1988), 'The economics of 1992', *European Economy*, Brussels.

Commission of the European Communities (1990), 'Social Europe', *European Economy*, Brussels.

Commission of the European Communities (1991), *Panorama of EC Industry 1991*, Brussels.

References

Commission of the European Communities (1992a), *Report of the Independent Experts on Company Tax (Ruding Committee)*, Brussels.

Commission of the European Communities (1992b), *Third Survey on State Aids in the European Community in Manufacturing and Certain Other Sectors*, Directorate General for Information, Brussels, July.

Coopers & Lybrand (1989), *Barriers to Takeovers in the European Community*, vol. 1, Study for the Department of Trade and Industry, HMSO, London.

Culem, Claudy (1988), 'Direct investments among industrialised countries', *European Economic Review*, 32.

Davis, Evan (1990), 'Synergies and the motivations for cross border merger', in *Continental Mergers are Different: Strategy and Policy for 1992*, London Business School, London.

de Ghellinck, Elisabeth (1991), 'The chemical and pharmaceutical industries', in D. Mayes (ed.), *The European Challenge: Industry's Response to the 1992 Programme*, Harvester Wheatsheaf, London.

Dicken, Peter (1992), *Global Shift: The Internationalisation of Economic Activity*, 2nd edn, The Guilford Press, London.

Dunning, John (1977), 'Trade, location of economic activity and the MNE: a search for an eclectic approach', in B. Ohlin, P.-O. Hesselborn, and P.M. Wijkman (eds), *The International Allocation of Economic Activity: Proceedings of a Nobel Symposium Held at Stockholm*, Macmillan, London.

European Economy, see Commission of the European Communities (1988 and 1990).

Forsgren, Mats, Ulf Holm and Jan Johanson (1992), 'Internationalisation of the second degree: the emergence of European-based centres in Swedish firms', in Stephen Young and James Hamill (eds), *Europe and the Multinationals*, Edward Elgar, Aldershot, Hants.

Geroski, Paul (1991), '1992 and European industrial structure', in G. McKenzie and A. Venables (eds), *The Economics of the Single European Act*, Macmillan, London.

Geroski, Paul, and Alexis Jacquemin (1985), 'Industrial change, barriers to mobility, and European industrial policy', *Economic Policy*.

Geroski, Paul, and Anastassios Vlassopoulos (1990), 'European merger activity: a response to 1992?', in *Continental Mergers are Different*, London Business School, London.

Gilchrist, Joseph, and David Deacon (1990), 'Curbing subsidies', in P. Montagnon (ed.), *European Competition Policy*, Royal Institute of International Affairs/Pinter, London.

Glickman, Norman, and Douglas Woodward (1989), *The New Competitors: How Foreign Investors are Changing the US Economy*, Basic Books, New York.

Graham, Edward (1978), 'Transatlantic investment by multinational firms: a rivalistic phenomenon', *Journal of Post-Keynesian Economics*, 1, Fall.

120

Greenaway, David (1987), 'Intra-industry trade, intra-firm trade and European integration', *Journal of Common Market Studies*, vol. XXVI.

Greenaway, David, and Robert Hine (1991), 'Intra-industry specialisation, trade expansion and adjustment in the European economic space', *Journal of Common Market Studies*, December.

Hager, Wolfgang, and Heimfried Wolf (1988), *The 'Cost of non-Europe': Obstacles to Transborder Business Activity*, Commission of the European Communities, Brussels.

Haigh, Robert, et al. (1989), *Investment Strategies and the Plant–Location Decision: Foreign Companies in the United States*, Praeger, New York.

Hölzer, Heinrich (1990), 'Merger control', in P. Montagnon (ed.), *European Competition Policy*, Royal Institute of International Affairs/Pinter, London.

Hood, Neil, and Thorsten Truijens (1992), 'European locational decisions of Japanese manufacturers: survey evidence on the case of the UK', Working paper 5–92, Business and Economic Studies on European Integration, Copenhagen Business School, Copenhagen.

International Monetary Fund (1977), *Balance of Payments Manual*, 4th edn, Washington, DC.

International Monetary Fund (1992), 'Final report of the working party on the measurement of international capital flows', Washington, DC, September.

Jacquemin, Alexis, and André Sapir (1988), 'International trade and integration of the European Community: an econometric analysis', *European Economic Review*, 32.

Julius, DeAnne (1990), *Global Companies and Public Policy: The Growing Challenge of Foreign Direct Investment*, Royal Institute of International Affairs/Pinter, London.

Julius, DeAnne, and Stephen Thomsen (1988), *Foreign Direct Investment among the G-5*, Discussion Paper No. 8, Royal Institute of International Affairs, London.

Kay, John (1990), 'Mergers in the European Community', in *Continental Mergers are Different*, London Business School, London.

Krugman, Paul (1985), 'Increasing returns and the theory of international trade', NBER Working Paper no. 1752, Cambridge, MA, October.

Krugman, Paul (1991), *Geography and Trade*, MIT Press, Cambridge, MA.

Kume, Gorota, and Keisuke Totsuka (1991), 'Japanese manufacturing investment in the EC: motives and locations', in Sumitomo Life Research Institute, *Japanese Direct Investment in Europe: Motives, Impact and Policy Implications*, Avebury, Aldershot, Hants.

Lim, Linda, and Pang Eng Fong (1991), *Foreign Direct Investment and Industrialisation in Malaysia, Singapore, Taiwan and Thailand*, OECD Development Centre, Paris.

London Business School (1990), *Continental Mergers are Different: Strategy and Policy for 1992*, London.

References

Mayes, D. (ed.), *The European Challenge: Industry's Response to the 1992 Programme*, Harvester Wheatsheaf, London.

McCulloch, Rachel (1988), 'International competition in services', in M. Feldstein (ed.), *The United States in the World Economy*, University of Chicago Press, Chicago.

McDermott, Michael (1992), 'The internationalisation of the South Korean and Taiwanese electronics industries: the European dimension', in S. Young and J. Hamill (eds), *Europe and the Multinationals*, Edward Elgar, Aldershot, Hants.

Molle, Willem, and Robert Morsink (1991), 'Intra-European direct investment', in B. Bürgenmeier and J. Mucchielli (eds), *Multinationals and Europe 1992*, Routledge, London.

Montagnon, Peter (1990), *European Competition Policy*, Royal Institute of International Affairs/Pinter, London.

Noble, Dorothea (1992), 'Industry dynamics in Europe: the motor industry', in S. Young and J. Hamill (eds), *Europe and the Multinationals*, Edward Elgar, Aldershot, Hants.

Organization for Economic Cooperation and Development (1985), *Economic Survey: Ireland 1984/85*, Paris.

Organization for Economic Cooperation and Development (1992a), *Foreign Direct Investment: Policies and Trends in the OECD Area during the 1980s*, Paris.

Organization for Economic Cooperation and Development (1992b), *Regulatory Reform, Privatization and Competition Policy*, Paris.

Organization for Economic Cooperation and Development (1992c), *Subsidies and Structural Adjustment*, Paris, May.

Porter, Michael (1987), 'From competitive advantage to corporate strategy', *Harvard Business Review*, 65, 3.

Reich, Robert (1991), 'Who is "Them"?', *Harvard Business Review*, March–April.

Ruding Committee, *see* Commission of the European Communities (1992a).

Sapir, André (1991), 'The structure of services in Europe: a conceptual framework', CEPR Discussion Paper 498, London, January.

Servan-Schreiber, J.-J. (1967), *The American Challenge*, translated from French by R. Steel, Hamish Hamilton, London.

Simões, Vitor (1992), 'European integration and the pattern of foreign direct investment inflow in Portugal', in J. Cantwell (ed.), *Multinational Investment in Modern Europe*, Edward Elgar, Cheltenham.

Thomsen, Stephen, and Phedon Nicolaides (1991), *The Evolution of Japanese Direct Investment in Europe: Death of a Transistor Salesman*, Harvester Wheatsheaf, London.

United Nations Centre on Transnational Corporations (1991), *World Investment Report 1991*, New York.

United Nations Centre on Transnational Corporations (1992), 'The determinants of foreign direct investment: a survey of the evidence', UNCTC Current Series, New York.

Wijkman, Per (1990), 'Patterns of production and trade', in W. Wallace (ed.), *The Dynamics of European Integration*, Royal Institute of International Affairs/Pinter, London.

Womack, J., D. Jones and D. Roos (1990), *The Machine that Changed the World*, Maxwell Macmillan International, Oxford.

Woodward, Douglas (1992), 'Locational determinants of Japanese manufacturing start-ups in the United States', *Southern Economic Journal*, vol. 58, no. 3, January.

Woolcock, Stephen (1989), *European Mergers: National or Community Control?*, Discussion Paper No. 15, Royal Institute of International Affairs, London.

World Bank (1991), *World Development Report 1991*, Washington, DC.

Yamawaki, Hideki (1991), 'Locational decisions of Japanese multinational firms in European manufacturing industries', mimeo, Department of Economics, Catholic University of Louvain.

Also in this series

Global Companies and Public Policy:
The Growing Challenge of Foreign Direct Investment

DeAnne Julius

'This book will help everyone who wants to understand how the world economy is changing and the implications for national policies. It calls into question some of the fundamental assumptions on which trade and exchange-rate policies are based.' – Peter B. Kenen, Princeton University.

'A magnificent piece of analysis. It shows how 1992 will lead to a new burst of cross-border activities, taking us beyond the traditional concepts of free trade and European integration. Essential reading for those who need to understand the globalization patterns that are likely to shape the economy of the early 21st century.' – Albert Bressand, Prométhée.

'This insightful book envisages and illustrates a world economy in the 1990s in which FDI-led market integration will effect enormous changes in economic relations among nations.' – Kiyohiko Fukushima, Nomura Research Institute.

'An imaginative yet careful treatment of a subject of great topical content to politicians, academics and businessmen. It deserves to be widely read.' – John H. Dunning, University of Reading.

The author
DeAnne Julius is Chief Economist at Shell International Petroleum Company and was formerly director of the International Economics Programme at the Royal Institute of International Affairs.

RIIA/PINTER PUBLISHERS

CHATHAM HOUSE PAPERS

Also in this series

European Competition Policy
edited by Peter Montagnon

Nowhere is the tension between Brussels and individual member states more evident than in the area of competition policy. This study examines the development of policy in four main areas: mergers and acquisitions, control of subsidies, the regulation of utilities, and the link between trade policy and competition policy. It tries to assess how well the Commission is equipped, in terms both of legal powers and of manpower resources, to deal with the issues involved. And, finally, it suggests that – on grounds of workload – there may be a case for creating a separate European authority to concentrate on merger policy. This is a controversial suggestion at present, but it is one which may have to be considered if a truly competitive environment for 1992 and beyond is to be secured.

Contents

The authors
Peter Montagnon is the World Trade Editor of *The Financial Times*. The book has been written in collaboration with Heinrich Hölzler (German Confederation of Industry), and Joseph Gilchrist and David Deacon of the EC Commission.

RIIA/PINTER PUBLISHERS

Also in this series

Global Financial Integration: The End of Geography

Richard O'Brien

New information technology is radically altering the ways in which financial markets interconnect. Even the location of markets has switched from physical trading floors to the more transient location of telephone and computer networks. Simultaneously a wave of regulatory change is sweeping through all financial markets, including the United States, Japan and Europe. These forces have helped liberate capital flows and 'end geography' in finance.

The author identifies thirteen key financial regulation items on the international agenda, all of critical importance to globalization and 'the end of geography'. From an analytical matrix he goes on to single out three areas requiring special attention: protecting consumers as cross-border financial services expand faster than anticipated; balancing the different ways in which financial systems link finance and commerce; and achieving a global framework for regulating banking, securities and insurance businesses.

Contents

1 Towards the end of geography; 2 Information technology and global finance; 3 The regulatory revolution; 4 The euromarket story: towards global banking; 5 Securities markets: big bangs across the globe; 6 The global retail challenge; 7 The lessons from Europe; 8 Everybody has to be somewhere: the new determinants of location; 9 Economic and political integration; 10 Summary and concluding recommendations

The author

Richard O'Brien is Chief Economist of American Express Bank Ltd. He is responsible for all economics research for the bank, worldwide, and is senior editor of *The AMEX Bank Review*.

RIIA/PINTER PUBLISHERS

CHATHAM HOUSE PAPERS

Also in this series

Market Access Issues in EC–US Relations: Trading Partners or Trading Blows?

Stephen Woolcock

In recent years transatlantic trade tensions have grown. The United States has viewed the European Community as creating a fortress, while Europe has looked on with increasing alarm at what it sees as a progressive shift in US policy from multilateralism towards unilateralism. These tensions have been exacerbated by conflicts over how to develop the multilateral trading system – as reflected in the heated negotiations in the GATT Uruguay round.

This study analyses the underlying issues behind such trade disputes. It discusses how open the two markets really are and what problems need to be overcome, and finds that, despite the bitter political battles, transatlantic economic interdependence continues to grow. Drawing on a number of key sectors, the study shows how the pace of this growth is being slowed by the lack of progress in providing the necessary policy framework within which transatlantic trade and investment should take place. There is therefore a danger of divergences developing that will threaten future growth.

The author
Stephen Woolcock is a Research Fellow with the European Programme of the Royal Institute of International Affairs. He was previously Deputy Director for International Affairs at the Confederation of British Industry, and has written widely on trade policy issues.

RIIA/PINTER PUBLISHERS